Teenage Triangle

Teenage Triangle

A Tale of Love Life and Optimism

ANUPAM SHAW

PARTRIDGE

A Penguin Random House Company

To order additional copies of this book, contact
Partridge India
000 800 10062 62
orders.india@partridgepublishing.com

www.partridgepublishing.com/india

Dedicated

to all my loving friends, parents, and teachers.

Acknowledgements

My sincere thanks to the following people for taking me ahead in my journey of writing this book.

First of all, thanks to my mom, Mrs Gayatri Devi, and dad, Mr Ashok Kumar Shaw, who always supported me directly or indirectly to bring out the author in me.

Mr R. C. Joshi, principal of L K SINGHANIA EDUCATION CENTRE. Sir, your inspirational classes are the only reason for my success, and moreover, only your precious words helped me take the initiative to write this book. I will never forget this line of yours:'Unless and until you prove your existence in this world, you are worthless.'

Rabi Kumar Mahapatra Sir and Dipti Maheswari Ma'am, whose support was always there with me in my hostel days which helped me to write this book.

Rishabh Banthia for reviewing this book for the very first time and even for helping me in deciding the title of the book.

At last if I am not thanking him then I am doing a big sin, yes he is Sumant Parakh who had helped me a lot in editing of the book.

I will also thank all those whom I may have missed mentioning here.

Prologue

'After ten years since we met, we have been the best of friends. Time flies away so quickly. The past has gone, never to come back, but it gifted us the sweet memories which still live in our hearts. Those memories of our childhood are our only friends in our lonely hour. We live with just a desire to relive our childhood days with our lovely friends, the days when we were all happy, with nothing to worry about and nothing to fear. May those times come back and give me one more day to enjoy with my friends.'

Akash spoke those words from his heart, and he brought out all his emotions in every word. There they were, those childhood best friends, meeting after ten years to relive those beautiful memories of their childhood. Those four best buddies were Akash, Anshika, Sumant, and Ananya.

'True, Akash, those were beautiful memories and are still vivid in my heart,' Sumant said.

'Akash is too emotional. Rona ajayega bas kar rahene de,' Ananya said.

'Yes, we are here to enjoy, not to cry over the gone past.' Anshika jumped in.

'But whatever you say, those were really the best days of my life. Now, they're just locked in my heart,' Akash said.

'It was really the best,' the others spoke in unison.

'Leave this entire thing. Akash, I was really confused about your love story—you and Anshika. How did it all get started? I have always wanted to ask you this but never got the chance. Anshika never spoke about her love story. Even being a best friend, she never shared with me your love story. Today I am not going to leave until I hear the whole story,' Ananya said.

Akash and Anshika were shying away from sharing their story, but Ananya's continuous insistence compelled Akash to relent.

'Okay, *babaa*, I am going to say it. Stop pleading.'

And the story began.

The First Best Friend

As I woke up, I heard the sound of a rooster (*kuukrrruuukuu . . .*) helping the village people to get up. I saw out from a little broken window of my hut that there was a red rooster making all the noise. And then I saw there were eight to ten buckets beside the tap and three naked children taking a bath. And the presence of eight to ten buckets means eight to ten more people will take a bath after those small children. I saw the time, which almost made me faint because it was six o'clock and I was already half an hour late. Every day I would get up at 5.30 a.m., and classes would start at 6.30 a.m. at the school, which was four kilometres far from my village, Chakdha.

'Akash, get up immediately and put your bucket there. Won't you take a bath?' Mom said.

I immediately got up, took a bucket from the veranda, and put it on the eleventh place. As I came back, it was 6.15 a.m. I was stunned after seeing the time; I immediately dressed up and went to school without even taking a bath and a dainty food which was cooked by Mom. While travelling in a local bus, I saw a guy who was also going to school, but he was talking in English on a mobile which was launched just few days back—Xiaomi MI3. He was well dressed and had a good physique, having six-pack abs, and a wristwatch on his hand. It seemed that he trains in a gymnasium. He had a bright, shining round face, was fair in complexion, and seemed to be part of a royal family. I knew my living standards couldn't be improved so easily because my father was a worker, but then I also didn't lose hope, and I set my goal to become a rich person.

After reaching the school, I attended the classes. As the classes ended, a teacher told me to submit the fees for this month, which was due because of our penury. As I came back home, I saw a new neighbour who came to the front of my house. They were also poor like us. I got a new friend who was of my age, and he even went to the same school as me. His name was Sumant, and we both were in the same class. The first day of our friendship passed very nicely just by interacting and playing with each other.

The First Impression

After waking up, I immediately went to Dad and told him about the fee which was due, and then I started getting ready for school. I went out and waited for Sumant.

'Hey! Morning,' Sumant said.

'A very good morning. Why are you so late on the first day, man?'

'Leave it, *yaar*. You just tell me, why are you smiling? What's the reason behind it?' he asked with an expression of interest.

'I am happy because of you.'

He looked at me with a confused stare. I explained, 'Actually, I used to get bored while travelling alone, but today you are here. That's why.'

'Oh, that's great. Let's go.'

The bus came, and we got in. I saw the same guy whom I had seen yesterday.

'Sumant, can you see that guy talking on his cell?'

'Yep.'

'Don't you think his clothes and his way of speaking seem that he is from a royal family?'

'Yeah, it seems so. But why you are asking such a question?'

'Because I want to have a lavish life.'

'Actually, I also want to live a life like that.'

We reached the school, still discussing. The first period was with Pranay Sir, who taught us Hindi. He came in, took attendance, taught, and went. The second period was with Bhatnakar Ma'am, who taught us history, one of the most monotonous subjects in the world. No one wanted to listen because the story was all about dead persons. But she came today and told us that after her period, we can go and play in the grounds because of the teachers' meeting.

We all came out in a jolly mood and decided to play a cricket match, and so the class was divided into teams with eleven members each. Luckily, Sumant was in my team. I was selected as the captain. The umpire tossed the coin; he was our Santosh dada (Santu da was his nickname), a club member of the Deshbandhu Club. Our team won the toss and decided to bat first. Ketan and Vinit were on the crease to bat.

The first ball of the first over was a massive four by Vinit, and Ketan also played in the same way. In the first over, we managed to do 11 runs. Their partnership ended after five overs when Vinit gave a catch at a silly point while trying to hook the bouncer from Suraj. And Ketan was also run out soon. After five overs, the score was 50 runs with the loss of 2 wickets.

Sumant and I were on the crease, and Sumant tried to accelerate; he pulled the first ball for a massive six, but later a swinging yorker from Suraj uprooted his middle stump. I didn't waste any time, and on a first ball, I struck a boundary followed by a huge six. The ball went outside the grounds. Soon, a new ball was taken. I intelligently took a single on the next ball. The score was now 67 for 3 in nine overs.

Dheeraj took the ball to bowl the third last over. I launched a massive six over the head of the medium pacer. With the next ball, I pulled it off again. It was a mishit; still it went all above the boundary. After three sixes in a row, I got carried away. I came out of the crease and tried to smash the ball hard, and it was a massive six over the head of the umpire.

The score table read 101 for 3 wickets. I completed my half century, and it was the last over for Suraj. Before the over began, I thought in my mind that in this over I had to hit 2 fours and a six, and I did it. And finally, we reached a winning score of 115 runs in twelve overs, and the opposite them needed 116 runs to win in their twelve overs.

I started proceeding. With the first ball, I bowled a perfect yorker, which Suraj played away with ease. The next two balls were dots; the fourth yorker ball of mine threw the middle stump, and Suraj was clean bowled. After the first over, the score was 4 runs for 1 wicket. Sumant took the ball for the second over, and he bowled a straight over for the batsman but lost 1 wicket.

The score reached 24 for 2 in the second over. I again came to bowl, but Suraj made a mockery of my yorker bowling and proved that I wasn't that quick. He hit me for 4 consecutive fours; the fifth ball, I bowled at him. After the end of three overs, the score was 40 for 4. The opponents batted wisely; they took single and double for the next five overs, and the score reached 70 for 8 in eight overs. The chase was still on, and suddenly our total looked small.

Ketan bowled a good over in between. He gave only 3 runs with a wicket in the same over. The match reached the final over. The scorecard read 100 runs for 9 wickets in eleven overs. They needed 16 runs in six balls with 7 wickets in the hand. Game could have gone anywhere until I bowled the last over.

I took the ball for the last over. I was confident, and I committed that I had to make this batsman out. With the first ball of the eleventh over, Rochis drove the ball to the cover, and it was a four. For the second ball of the eleventh over, Rochis came out of the crease and drove the ball over my head for a six. Suddenly, the match seemed to be slipping from our hands.

I looked at the sky, and from inside my soul, I said that I could and I would make this Rochis bowled in this ball. And I threw a swinging yorker which uprooted his middle stump. And finally, we won the match. The supporters and our team members started dancing on the pitch. After the fabulous game, we went to class, took our bags, and left for home.

As we got down from the bus, I saw Santu da.

'Hello, Santu da. For whom are you waiting here?' I asked.

'I am fine and waiting for you both only.'

'For us, but why? Just a few minutes back, we were still on the grounds. What has become so important for you to come here?'

'I am here just to praise you both.'

'What? You came here just to praise us? You could have just praised us there,' I said.

'I came here not to praise you only but to give you both prizes also.'

'Prizes! Wow.'

'Yah, just because first, I have not seen guys who plays as good as you both. You have done a great job. At such a young age, you both have played in such a way that was marvellous.

That's why I came here to give the prizes only to you both. And the prize is a cash award of 500 rupees to both of you.'

'Oh . . . that's nice. Thank you very much, Santu da. Now with this money I will buy all those things which I don't have,' Sumant said.

'And you, Akash, what will you do with this money? Hey, why are you crying? Have I hurt you?' Santu da said.

'No, these are tears of happiness. Instead of spending it, I will give this money to my father. As you know, dada, we belong to a middle-class family so, a penny saved is a penny earned for us.'

'Awesome. What positive thinking you have. If I were in your place, I would have spent it at all. One thing I would like to say is that your thoughts are really very good.'

'Thank you, dada, for praising me.'

'Oh, please don't thank me. I have told you only those things which I had seen in you, and instead of thanking me, you should thank your parents, who had taught you in such a manner that today you think twice before taking each step.'

'Yah, it's true. I will thank them also.'

'Now I have got to go. We will meet later. Bye-bye . . . and have a nice day,' dada said.

I entered my home and saw that Dad was talking to Mom.

'Hey, Dad, there's good news. I want to give you something today.'

'What is it that you want to give me?'

'The gift is 500 rupees. And this is for you only.'

'Where did you get it from?'

'Dad, Santu da gave it to me as a prize. I hope you know him. He is a club member of our Deshbandhu Club.'

'No, I don't. Okay, leave it. You just tell me why he gave you a prize. I can't understand the reason.'

'Dad, actually there was a cricket match today in which our team won the match. We played so nicely that our team won the match, and that's why he gave us the prizes. And Santu da told us that he is giving us the prizes just because he hadn't seen in his life someone at such a young age who can play so nicely.'

Dad praised me, and then after dinner, I went to sleep.

Impact of Cricket

The next day as I woke up, my mother served me a delicious breakfast. After taking it, Sumant and I went to school together. As soon as we entered the classroom, everybody started praising us for our play yesterday.

Someone even told me, 'Akash, the way you hit the massive sixes and fours on every other ball, your name should be Sehwag.'

'Please, guys, even all of you can do that with some practice, and don't praise me so much that in the next match, I won't even hit a single four.'

'We are not praising you at all. We are just telling the truth. And Sumant, the way you fielded, it was simply awesome, bro!'

Pranay Sir entered the class.

'Good morning, students.'

'Good morning, sir.'

'Why are you all standing here?'

'Sir, Akash and Sumant are very good players,' Ketan said.

'What do you mean by good players? What do you want to say?'

'Sir, yesterday there was a cricket match, and in that game, the way they played was simply awesome. You missed it.'

'Did they play so well that you are all praising them so much?'

'We cannot even explain it, sir. That's the reason we are saying that you missed it,' Vinit said.

'Okay, if you all are praising them so much, then Akash and Sumant, be ready for one more match. You both have to play tomorrow in front of the entire administrative staff.'

As the school ended, we met our friends and started chit-chatting.

'Guys, you shouldn't have praised us so much. What if tomorrow we lose the match?'

'Chill out, bro. We all know that you both can play well, and tomorrow you will kick everyone's arses,' Ketan said.

The next day, as we went to play the match, the team had already been selected. We won the toss and selected to bat first. Sumant and I were single-handedly able to reach a winning score of 130 runs in a quota of twelve overs. I scored 70 out of forty-two balls, in which I hit 4 sixes and 8 fours. And Sumant's score was 60 out of thirty balls.

We bowled well and won the match. Sumant took 4 wickets by giving only 10 runs, and I took a single wicket. Sumant and I were given prizes by Pranay Sir, who was totally surprised after seeing our match.

Surprise

The next day, as I entered the class, Pranay Sir asked me, 'Akash, do you know the person who was the umpire of yesterday's match?'

'Yah, I know him, but why are you asking about him?'

'Nah, just simply tell me where he lives.'

'He lives just beside our house, sir. His name is Santosh, and we call him Santu da, he is a member of the Deshbandhu Club.'

'What?'

'Yes, sir, but why are you staring at me with wide eyes?'

'No, it's nothing, you can proceed to your class.'

In his mind, Pranay Sir thought, *Is he that Santosh who used to be my classmate? Is he that guy whom we used to call Champu, a duffer in studies but a star in cricket? If he is the same guy, then will he be able to recall his memories after seeing me, those funny days we spent together? Will he be able to recognize me?* A lot of questions were unfurling in Pranay Sir's mind, but they couldn't be solved until and unless he met him. As per the given address, he reached there to Santu da's place.

'Hey, Champu! How are you? Do you remember who I am?'

Santu started staring at Pranay and was giving him a blank stare as if he was a stranger to him.

'Ohhhh! Rattu [mugger], is that you? Where have you been lately? Is everything fine? How did you come to know my address?'

11

A lot of questions were asked and a lot were answered by him within a second.

'Well, Akash told me. Actually, I only asked him about the umpire, but I did not know that it was only you. When he mentioned your name, at that time I started wondering whether it was you or somebody else, but luckily, it was you.'

'Okay, but why?'

'Actually, I want to give them a surprise.'

'Surprise! What kind of surprise?'

'Actually, I thought that the umpire is a member of the Deshbandhu Club, which obviously is you, and for sure he must have his own cricket team. And if he can include Akash and Sumant in his team, then their talents will not remain hidden. Who knows? They may get selected for the district, state, nationals, or maybe for the international front also. Do you agree with my views?'

'Yes, obviously, there is going to be a match soon, and I will make sure they play well in it.'

'Thanks, yaar, but please don't tell them about this. It is going to be a surprise for them.'

Shocking News

The next day, as we entered our school, our hands came over our mouths after hearing that our final exams have been preponed. I was totally dumbstruck by this horrible news because I hadn't even touched my books till date. There was only a month left, and I had to study eight subjects.

'Hey, Sumant, what about studies?'

'Don't ask, dude. It is in the down lanes. I even don't know the subjects of the chapters that are going to come out. Please help me.'

'Let's do one thing. In the evening, I will come to your place. We will start our preparation together. I will be there by six o'clock.'

In the evening as I entered his home, I saw him studying, which made me totally freeze.

'Hey, Sumant, what's going on?'

'Nothing frivolous. It's biology.'

'Bio—ohh, wow! That means you are interested in this subject. That's great. Which topic are you reading? What's this? I haven't seen this topic in my book.'

'You didn't see it because it's not in our books.'

'What? Then why are you wasting your time reading it?'

'Arré, it is really interesting. Just read this particular topic about women's boobs. See the image? It's a hemispherical shape.'

'Fuck you, asshole! You will never stop all this, will you? Exams are on heads, and all you are interested in is about boobs. "Hemispherical boobs", seriously? If you are really interested in such things, then purchase those magazines which have nude girls in them. At least, don't insult these books.'

'Really? Such magazines are available in the market?'

'Yeah, obviously.'

'Wow! I want some of those then.'

'Please keep your mouth shut. Don't even try to see those magazines.'

'What? But why? In the first place, you were the one who told me about this entire thing, and now you are trying to become so innocent as if you don't know anything about all this.'

'Oh please, I am not trying to become innocent. It's my habit to keep knowledge of each and every thing. Leave it, yaar, let's just study mathematics.'

'Yeah, okay, fine. The first chapter is on the number system, but the word problems are tough.'

'Please, Sumant, don't start thinking negatively at the beginning itself. If you think that it's hard, then the easy questions will also seem hard, and you won't be able to solve a single question also. Always remember one thing in your life: there are solutions to every problem in life if you think there's a way.'

'Wow! Aaa gaye babaji.'

After spending an hour with him, I came back home.

Good News

The next day as we both reached school, we were briefed by Pranay Sir, who called us into the staff room and told us that he wanted both of us to go watch the final match between India and Sri Lanka.

'Beta, there's a World Cup match between India and Sri Lanka on 2 April 2011. I will get tickets for you to go and watch the match in the stadium because I think you both have great potential, and after seeing the match, I think that you can improve your performance.'

'Oh thanks, sir, you are really one of the best teachers I have ever known,' I said.

'So nice of you, sir. Thank you very much.'

'Yah, it's okay. Now go back to your class. I'm coming within a minute,' Pranay Sir said.

'Hey, Akash, don't you think that Pranay Sir really thinks too well about our interests?'

'Yah, you are right.'

'Akash, I think that we should improve our academic performance also. If our academic results will be good, then I think Pranay Sir's interest towards our well-being will get paid off. And anyhow in the end, the ultimate profit will be ours.'

'Yah, it's true. By the way, be ready today for the next chapter in maths. I will be there by six o'clock in the evening. Bye-bye,' I said.

Dream

After coming home from school, I set the alarm and slept, but as the alarm rang at five in the evening, I woke up and realized that I had been dreaming. It was a nice one, I must say. I saw Sumant, who was searching for a magazine in a busy market, but I didn't know exactly where it was.

At last, he succeeded in finding the magazine, and he bought it. On the cover page of the magazine, there was a pic of a half-naked girl wearing only pink panties and covering her boobs by pressing her nipples with her hands. Half of her boobs were visible. They appeared hemispherical in shape just like those which I saw on that day in that book, and the expression on her face was so sexy that even I wanted to have a peek in the magazine. I mean, people say never judge a book by its cover; today I ask all those people, will you not judge such a magazine by its cover page?

Sumant had just started looking at the content when in the midst of the crowd, I saw a girl. She was really beautiful. I fell in love with her instantly. I don't know whether it was the surroundings or the time, but I knew one thing for sure that I was getting lost. That smile, those beautiful glittering eyes—oh god! The way she was arguing with the veggie vendor. Man, this girl was gorgeous. I felt as if I had seen an angel. Yes, she was an angel—my angel . . .

As I stepped forward to go and speak with her, the alarm rang. This stupid thing, I really hate it. It always rings at the wrong time.

Preparation

When I reached Sumant's place, I saw him reading the newspaper and smiling.

'Hey, Sumant, why do you have that mischievous smile on?'

'It's the news, bro, which is making me smile. Read it, you will also smile. Leave it. You see this pic?'

'What's wrong? Such an innocent face she has, and you are smiling at her.'

'You fool! I am smiling because of the headline. The headline says that if India wins the World Cup, then she will strip in front of all the cricket players.'

'What are you saying? Have you gone insane? An Indian girl and striping! Not at all possible.'

'Yah, Akash, I can understand your feelings. You are saying that these types of girls who are speaking about stripping will not look good. After all, the *firangs* [foreigners] are always a treat to watch in such acts.'

'Hello, mister. I didn't mean that.'

'But whatever your perception may be, for me she is very hot. If she strips in front of me, then only God knows what will happen to me, but I can imagine the situation.

'Arz kiya hai

Iss duniya mein hassenayein kam hai

Waqt ki pabandi se ham band hai

Yaad rakhna aae duniya walon

Hamare andar dam na kisi se kam hai.'

'Sumant, can you please stop this shit? You know I don't like it.'

'Can't you just imagine the situation for my sake? I know that you are a voyeur.'

'I don't want to study with you. I'm going. Bye.'

'*Arré*, sorry, *yaar*! Sorry! Come back and chill down, man. I will not speak about it again, I promise.'

'You can talk about it, but only to some extent. Leave it. Just clean the mess, and let's study the next chapter, probability.'

'Akash, I think it's a very interesting chapter, and we can understand it very easily.'

'Hmm okay . . . the first question is: "A lad tossed the coin once. What is the probability of getting heads?"'

'The answer is simple: the probability is one-half. Am I right?'

'Yah, dude, but how do you know how to do this?'

'Let's say, for example, I say that tomorrow I'm going to buy the magazine. If I buy it, then what is the probability of me getting caught at home? The answer is one-half because the total number of members in my home who don't know about the magazine are two—Mom and Dad—and the magazine is one. So it will be either my mom or my dad who will catch me, not anyone else. Thus, the probability is half. Got it?'

'Yah, bro. Sumant, I will never forget you in my whole life. The way you relate things is awesome. I can't even think of relating probability to those magazines.'

'Please, that's enough. Let's do the sum,' said Sumant and gave me a smirk.

'Yah . . . I came here to do the sums only, but you always start gossiping, which wastes our time. By the way, be ready for tomorrow. I hope you remember that tomorrow we have to go watch the World Cup match after school. The match will start at 2.30 p.m.'

'Yes, dude, I remember it.'

First Glimpse of Players

I was very much excited because of the match that I had to witness today in the stadium. As we reached school, Pranay Sir met us and told us to meet him after the last period. Sumant and I were just waiting for the last period to end. And as the last period ended, our chests puffed up just because of the excitement of seeing all the cricket players in reality in front of our eyes.

Earlier we used to see them on TV, but now, we will get t see them in real life. As we met Pranay Sir, he gave us the tickets to the Wankhede Stadium in which the seat numbers were written, and he even gave us 500 rupees for other related expenses. After coming home from school, we immediately changed our clothes, took our lunch, and rode the bus for the Wankhede Stadium. After travelling for one hour, we finally reached the stadium. As we reached near the entrance gate, we saw there was a long queue. Thousands of young people were standing and were hooting for the Indian team. Some were busy buying the flags and caps for India, some had their faces painted with the colours symbolizing the names of the players and the country, and some of the lads were even half exposed and had the flag of India painted on their bodies.

After waiting for an hour, our turn came, and we entered the stadium. As we entered, we were stunned to see the grounds. It was so big that we cannot even imagine how much power would be required to hit fours and sixes on these grounds. We occupied our seats, which was just diagonal to the stage, where cheerleaders would dance. We were just watching all around the grounds to get a glimpse of any players, but we couldn't find anyone.

At 2 p.m. everyone started yelling like anything just because Dhoni, Sangakkara, and the umpire arrived on the grounds to toss the coin. India won the toss and chose to bowl first. After half an hour, the match started, and in the first over, a four was smashed. Every one of the supporters of the Sri Lankan team started yelling and showing the flag of their country, and even the cheerleaders of the Sri Lankan team came on the stage and started dancing and jumping.

From the place where Sumant and I were seated, the match was not clearly visible because the pitch was too far away, but the cheerleaders were very visible because they were closer and diagonal to us. They were wearing miniskirts and brassieres. Sri Lanka was not our team, but then if they hit fours and sixes, Sumant would become happy and start chuckling. I did not know the reason behind it. I noticed him do it once, twice, and thrice. I ignored him, but again on the fourth time when he started chuckling, I lost my patience and asked him the reason behind it.

'Why have you been smiling for the last half an hour and even only after fours or sixes? Are you getting excited when the opposite team is smashing fours and sixes?'

'No way. How can I be happy if another team plays well? There's another reason behind that, and I can't share it. If I will say it, then you will be angry.'

'I promise I will not be angry. You just share it with me. I also want to laugh.'

'I am laughing just because two melons are fighting each other to get adjusted in a small satchel and even one melon or other is coming out, showing half its body, and then going back.'

'What are you saying? I don't understand.'

'I mean to say that whenever the fours or sixes are smashed by the batsman, the cheerleaders start jumping and dancing, and their boobs move in such a way you cannot even imagine. Instead of *melons*, put *boobs*, and you can understand the situation.'

'Sumant, you are so . . . Here also you are staring there instead of watching the matches. You should feel shame.'

'There's nothing to be ashamed of. Nobody is gazing at me or cares what I'm doing. Then what's wrong there? I can gaze at those cheerleaders—at least, at their melons.'

'Leave this entire thing and watch the match. Oh yes, the first wicket fell down, and the scoreboard reads 17 for 1 in 6.1 overs.'

After completing fifty overs in two and a half hours, the scoreboard read 274 for 6, and all the players started going back to the restroom. We also felt hungry because we hooted for our team to the fullest, and we decided to leave the place in search of victuals so that in the next half, we would have more energy to hoot for our India team when they do bat. As we reached the stall, we decided to buy cakes, chips, and soft drinks to boost up our energy level. While consuming our foodstuff, Sumant got a glimpse of a magazine stall, and he took me there after finishing the food.

'Akash, you were right, yaar. Here I can see those magazines which you told me. They're available in the market. Please suggest to me which one I should buy and in which magazine there will be pics of fully exposed women.'

'Oh, *bhai*, do you think I am the owner of this shop or that I had published these magazines?'

'I think you are neither the shopkeeper nor the publisher.'

'Then why are you asking me? Ask the person who is selling.'

'No way. How can I ask him? He is of my father's age.'

'Then let's go. I cannot explain it to you, and you cannot ask him. Then why waste time?'

'Wait, wait. I can ask. Uncle, can I see these magazines?'

'Beta, it's not the right place to see it. If you will look at it here, everyone will start gazing at you. And you are even a kid, so it's better for you to buy it and keep it aside,' the uncle replied.

'Akash, I think I should buy the one with Pamela. See how she covers her boobs with her hands?'

'I don't know. As you wish.'

He bought the suggested magazine.

'Sumant, put this magazine in your right hand and cover the magazine's cover page with your body and then walk normally.'

'Yes, you are right, but Akash, why is everyone gazing at me?'

'Oh shit! Sumant, there is a pic of a naked woman on the back cover, and this is the reason they are gazing. Put this magazine inside your vest. This is the only right place to hide it.'

'What? Really, Akash? It has been truly said that dealing with the wrong thing is very difficult.'

At last we reached our seats, and the match was going to start.

'Akash, see the pics of Pamela? They're nice. Look at her boobs.'

'Sumant, stop this nonsense and watch the match. Sehwag and Sachin are on the crease, and Sehwag is on the strike. The match is going to start soon. Wow! Good shot played, and a single run was taken by Viru. Sumant, can you see how calmly they are playing just by striking the ball and taking single runs? Oh shit, one wicket fell, and Viru got out just by scoring 2 runs. Oh god, what's going on? Help us. If India will play in this way, then we will lose the match.'

'Akash, don't be tense. Our Cricket God is on the ground, the Master Blaster.'

'Yah, I think he will manage it. Wow! Awesome shot by Blaster. It's four,' I said.

'See, Akash? I told you, when Blaster is there, no one should be tense.'

'Hmm. Oh shit. Gone, India. Gone,' I said.

'What?'

'If you will gaze at the magazine, then how will you know what's going on in the cricket game? I mean to say, Sachin is also out by scoring 18 runs. And will you please stop gazing at the magazine? Otherwise, you will not be able to take an interest in the World Cup match.'

'Yah, I think you are right. I should watch the match because it's getting interesting. Wow! Awesome four by Gambhir. Akash, now only Gambhir, Dhoni, Kohli, and Yuvraj are left to control the match because they are batsmen. If they can't play well, then India will lose the match.'

After forty-five overs, my heartbeat increased just because of fear. The match could be won by any team. Forty-five overs had passed, and India had lost 3 wickets and is not even leading. The remaining balls and runs were nearly equal.

'Oh shit! Sumant, Gambhir is out at 97. He would be feeling so bad; if he would be able to score 3 more runs, then he would have done centuries.'

'Yah, that's true, Akash, but now India had lost 4 wickets. Dhoni and Yuvraj are there on the crease.'

'Sumant, don't you think Dhoni is smashing helicopter shots today? And he is even showing the responsibility of captainship in the right time and on the right day.'

'Hmm.'

'Sumant, we have come to the end of the match. India needs 4 runs in eleven balls. Wow! Fabulous six by Dhoni, and the scoreboard reads 277 for 4 in 48.2 overs. We have won the match, Sumant!'

'Yah, Akash, see those rockets in the sky? It seems like today is Deepawali.'

'Of course, yaar, India has won the World Cup match. For India, that's like Deepawali. Sumant, I also want to be a cricketer like them, and I even want to play with Viru in the same field.'

'I also want to play with Kohli because I am a fan of his.'

'Hmm, great. I really feel very happy to know that today there are still youths who think about sports. Otherwise, most of them want to become doctors, engineers, CAs, or they want to get a job in good MNCs. Beta, I want you to be there. Best of luck for your future, and start practising,' said the uncle who was sitting in front of us.

'Thank you, uncle,' we said.

'No problem, dude. We can and will play with them. "We are born to win and to be a winner we must prepare to win. Then only we can expect to win."'

Clash among Friends

After reaching school the next day, we first met Pranay Sir and thanked him once again and even shared our experiences with him.

When we entered the class, Sumant cried, 'Dude, I am in trouble.'

'What trouble?'

'*Arré*, the magazine which I bought yesterday, I left it under my pillow. I forgot to hide it. When my mom sets the bed, she will surely see that magazine.'

'What? Sumant, you will get me also in trouble with you.'

'How will you be in trouble, man?'

'When your parents will start beating you, you will start uttering the truth, and I know at that time you will even tell my name and also the fact that I told you about the magazine. But I will not accept that. I am telling you in advance.'

'What? But why?'

'Because I didn't ask you to buy it. I just gave you information that in the market this type of magazine is also available.'

'Okay, no problem, dude. When my mom will complain to your mom that you provided me this type of knowledge instead of helping me study, then you will also be beaten.'

'Okay, let's see who will be kicked out, you or me. Bye-bye,' I said.

Sumant thought, *Will I be able to face Mom's anger? Will I be able to convince her? Will she agree with my excuses or will I be kicked out? Can these excuses help me, like by saying that it was due to Akash that I indulged in this entire thing, or will she simply slap me? And then there will be the same question, if Akash is going to jump in the well, then will I also jump?* A lot of questions started running in his mind.

After school, Sumant prayed and entered the room. He saw his bed was set, and there was no magazine under his pillow. He knew that it could have only been taken by his mom. He peeped inside the kitchen to see his mom. She was howling while cooking food. He understood the reason behind her weeping. He didn't utter a single word and went back to his room to change and then started studying maths. Soon his mother entered the room.

'Oh, trying to act innocent?' his mom said.

'What? Actually, Mom, exams are on our heads. That's why.'

'Oh, so sincere you are. By the way, what did you do yesterday night?'

'Me?'

'Yah, I am talking to you only,' she said it with such anger that I was sure that today Deepawali was gonna be celebrated.

'Hmm. Mom, I slept early yesterday night because of exhaustion.'

Smash! She placed a tight hit on my face.

'You stupid, telling lies to your mom. Then what is this, and whose magazine is this? Watching pics of naked girls, such a brazen lad you are. I can't even imagine that my son would be like this. I should bow my head that I have given birth to you.'

'Sorry, Mom.'

'What sorry? At first, doing such a nonsense thing, then telling a lie, and now you are saying sorry? You will get a punishment.'

'Okay, Mom. I am ready, but please don't say this thing to Dad. Please, Mom.'

'Okay. Then your punishment is that you will not go out to play or anything except to your school till the exams are over.'

'What? But, Mom—'

'But what? You have only two options—either I will tell your father about this or you agree with the punishment.'

'No way! I am agreeing with the punishment only.'

'Hmm,' Mom said.

The next day, Sumant met me while going to school. I grinned and asked him, 'How are you?'

'I am fine.'

'Tell the story.'

'Well, Mom saw it. She was crying and really pissed off. She also gave me a punishment that I can't go out to play or anything else till the exams end, but luckily, she didn't ask me from where I got it. Well, let's leave this entire thing. I think we have already wasted and enjoyed the last month. Our exams are going to start tomorrow, and the first one is on history. I don't understand why we should learn about the people who have already died. Will you please come to my home after taking supper? We will discuss the chapter, and then we will learn it.'

When I reached his home, he was already reading the chapter on Mohenjo-Daro.

'Hey,' I said.

'Thank God you came here. Please teach me something. I can't even understand a single line. Someone has said rightly that history is the subject which has to be crammed as no one can understand it.'

'Correct. Then why did you call me? You know that it needs mugging power. Just mug it up.'

'Bro, I don't have a cramming power like you.'

'Please don't tell me that. I was not born with an extra brain. You can also do it, you are no less than anyone else.'

'You are really nice, yaar. Thank you for motivating me.'

'Yah, yah, best of luck. Prepare it nicely. I am going back home.'

After Exams

The bell rang, and after our last exam, we came out of the class with big smiles on our faces.

'Hey, Sumant, how were the exams?'

'Awesome. My maths exam is always good because it's my favourite subject, you know.'

'Dude, don't you think we've worked hard for the last two weeks? Today our exams are over, so why not play a match?' I said.

'Yep, why not? My mom will also permit me to go out because our exams are over now.'

After coming home, I immediately rushed to the grounds to play the match; it seemed as if I got bailed because living at home and studying 24/7, it's better to call it a jail rather than a home. I even saw Santu da and requested him to be the umpire. As usual, our team won the match, and again Santu da was happy with our performance.

The next day, after teaching in class, Pranay Sir called us into the staff room and told us to be ready for the surprise.

'My next gift is that you have to play a match again. This time, not in school, but in Janardhan Ground, and you are even included in Santosh da's cricket team. Tomorrow there is going to be a match, and you are going to play with the Sporting Club cricket team. And if you play well there, then you may get a chance to get selected for a district team. I hope you know that Sporting Club is one of the famous clubs in our district, so be ready, and best of luck for the match.'

'Thank you, sir, thanks a lot. But, sir, I still have a doubt as to when I was included in Santu da's cricket team. He didn't tell us anything,' I said.

'Yes, I only told him not to say just to give you a surprise. And on that day, when I saw that the way you both played was awesome, I didn't have any second thoughts. I immediately called you and asked you about Santu da because I knew that he has his own cricket team. I even told him to include you both in his team, and he agreed.'

'You have made such big plans for us,' Sumant said.

'Yah. Okay, leave this entire thing, and ha, best of luck for tomorrow,' Pranay Sir said.

'Thank you, sir. Thank you very much,' we said.

'Sumant, don't you think our dreams are coming into reality?'

'Yah, God always helps those who do hard work. By the way, tomorrow we have to rock the stadium.'

'Yes, dude.'

The bell rang, and we went out of the school, swinging our arms because of the excitement that we were getting a chance to get selected for district tournaments. We immediately took lunch and went back to the grounds for practice.

Next day as we reached there, we saw everyone was waiting for us. We quickly joined our team, and we had an introduction to the head of the Sporting Club. His hands even came over his mouth when we introduced ourselves because we were too small for that team. And there was only one question in his mouth—whether we would be able to play with them or not. But Santu da quickly told him to just wait and watch our performance and our confidence level.

Then the coach introduced himself as Ajeet Singh Rajpurohit. The coin was tossed, and we decided to bowl first. Our whole team was on the ground to begin the match, and I was ready with the new ball to start a new over. The match began, and in the first over, I took a wicket by giving 3 runs. In the second over, Sumant took a wicket by giving only a single run. In the same way, I took a wicket in the third, seventh, ninth, and tenth overs. And Sumant also took it in the fourth, fifth, sixth, and eighth overs. It was only in ten overs that the opposition was all out, and their score was just 84. Santu da looked really happy with our performance in bowling. As we started batting, most balls were fours and sixes. Not even a single player was able to uproot our stump; everyone got exhausted, and we finished the game in just 7 overs.

At last, Ajeet Sir himself decided to bowl to uproot our stump. But before his bowling, I called Sumant and told him not to smash the ball. If we smash it, then Ajeet Sir will lose his dignity, and if while playing, he uprooted our stump, then our dignity will be lost. So it's better to smash a single four and then just go for strike for two to three balls and then get out.

As per the plan, Sumant was on the strike; for the first ball, he struck it; second four, third strike; and on fourth ball, instead of going for a lower cut, he knowingly moved the bat upwards for an upper cut to uproot his stump, then he was out. I also did it in the same way, and I was out. We both were out in just eight balls. All the players started howling and enjoying a lot. But Ajeet Sir understood that we got out by our own wish.

He said to us, 'I can understand your feelings. You both are really good in nature. You thought of my dignity, and that's why you didn't hit the ball. Great, you both are selected for the district team, and from now onwards, you will play for our team.'

'Thank you, sir. Thank you very much.'

'Please don't say thanks. If I were in your place, then I would have simply smashed more sixes so that the selector would have thought thrice before throwing the ball. But your thoughts were the opposite, and that is nice, keep it up.'

'Santu, your players are really good,' he said to Santu da.

'Yah, that's why I told you to just wait and watch.'

'By the way, in which school do they read?'

'In Nagar Vidyalaya.'

'What? They are students of a Hindi-medium school?'

'Yah. Why are you so shocked?'

'Arré, yaar, they should read in an English-medium school. A cricket player must have a good command of English. They should speak it fluently. These guys who play so well are the future of India, and they are in a government school—'

'But, Ajeet, they are financially weak.'

'So what? Tell them that for the next academic session, they should get admitted to an English-medium school because as you know, our club pays the players, so for them, we will pay the school fees instead of giving them money. But they should learn and work hard both in games and academics. By the way, Santu, it's getting late, we have to go now. I will talk to you later. Goodbye.'

The next day, when we both entered the school, everyone gathered around us, and it seemed like we had become celebrities. Everyone knew that we had been selected for the district team by the *Sporting Club*. Pranay Sir entered the class.

'Students, please be quiet. I know you all are very much excited, but there's also bad news for us.'

'What?'

'Yes, students. Starting from the next academic session, Sumant and Akash will no longer be with us.'

'No longer be with us? What do you mean, sir?' I said.

'I mean that Ajeet Sir, who had selected you for the district team, wants you both to read in an English-medium school because a cricket player must have a good command of English. And that's why, on the next academic session, you will have to leave the school.'

After teaching in his period for thirty minutes, he told me and Sumant to follow him to the staff room.

'Akash and Sumant, I know you are thinking how it would be possible for you to read in a private school when the only private school here is too expensive, am I correct?'

'Yes, sir.'

'Don't worry. Ajeet had told Santu that his club will pay the fees for you both. The amount which you both are paying now, you will only have to pay the same amount, and the remaining fees will be paid by the club. And moreover, I should make one thing clear. The club is not donating money. They usually pay the players who play for their team. Instead of paying you the amount, they will pay your fees, and even if you ask for money for day-to-day expenses, you can also get it.'

'Thanks, sir, and also please thank him for us,' I said.

'I think that cricket will change our whole lives,' said Sumant as soon as we left the staff room.

Results

As we stepped inside the class, we saw Pranay Sir distributing the answer sheets.

'Sir, may I get in?' I asked.

'Yah, come in. I was only waiting for you. See what you have done. How many marks were you expecting? Do you think that you will be able to get admission in that private school with such marks?'

A lot of questions were bombarded at us one after another with frivolous anger, to which we had no answer.

Pranay Sir said, 'Akash, you have scored only 80 per cent. And Sumant, your percentage is lower than his. You have scored only 75 per cent. I can't understand how you both can play so well but be so slow in academics. In this competitive world, the percentage which you have secured is not going to work at all. This time, you are getting admission into St. Xavier's Institution, but after school, with such percentages, you will not get admission into any college. So please start studying so that at least you can secure good marks and you do not have to face any problems after your school life.' After saying all this, he turned towards the class.

'Yes, students, return the answer sheets and listen. Our next class will be on 10 March, and you will get your results on that day.'

'Sumant, will you tell your parents about the results today?' I said.

'No way. Are you mad? Today I will tell my parents that I have been selected as a district player in the club and that I am also going to get paid for it. I didn't say it on that day, and I will even tell them that I am getting admission into Xavier's as a gift. They will be very happy after hearing these. I will only show the results on 10 March. What about you?'

'I am also going to do the same thing, and what will happen after that, only God knows.'

When I reached home, I was already nervous because of my low marks. But then I tried to overcome the nervousness by bringing a smile to my face and then stepped inside.

'Mom, there's good news for you.'

'Good news?'

'Yah, Mom, your son has been selected for the district team.'

'District team means . . . ?'

'It means that to achieve any goal, there are certain stages which we have to achieve, and then finally we are able to accomplish that goal. In the same way, cricket has some stages, and this is the first one. Actually, we had a cricket match in which Sumant and I played so nicely that we had been selected for the district team, and if we play well in that, then we will get selected for state, then national, and then Ranji. And if we will play well in Ranji, then we will be in an international match along with Sachin, Sehwag, and others.'

'What are you saying? Really. It's hard to believe, but it's very interesting news.'

'Yah, Mom. It's interesting news, but where is Dad?'

'I'm just here. What happened, and why are you both so happy?'

'Dad, I have been selected for the district team!'

'What? But who selected you?'

'Dad, he is the head of the Sporting Club, who came to witness the match between his team and Santu da's team. In the beginning, he was not sure about me and Sumant because according to him, we were too small to play the match, but after seeing us play in the field, he was shocked. He decided to include us in his team. I have one more good news. Starting from the next academic session, I will be studying in an English-medium school.'

'But how?'

'Dad, when the cricket coach came to know that we read in a Hindi-medium school, he immediately told Santu da that you will only have to pay the fee which you are paying now for me and the remaining amount will be paid by the club. Because he thinks that it is important for the cricket players to have a good command of English. And the second most important thing is that we are the youths of the nation, and we should not lag behind in any field. And the third reason is that we have played so well in a mind-blowing game that he was impressed, and that's why he told us that if we will play for his team, then instead of giving us money, the club will pay the school fees for us.'

'Hmm! It's really good news for today.'

A Week Later

'Sumant, tomorrow our results are going to be declared.'

'Yah, I am afraid, bro. What will happen?'

'But why? We already know the results.'

'The problem is that tomorrow we have to show our results to our parents. What will we say if they ask about the answer sheets?'

'Hmm. But Sumant, I don't think they will be so angry.'

'You don't know my dad. He is really short-tempered.'

'Don't worry. I know you can flatter your parents, and even I am also going to do that.'

After getting the results, l started staring at it with wide eyes just by seeing my marks in maths. I secured 48 out of 100 and had failed by just two marks; the marks were underlined by a red pen. The school had a rule that the paper of the subject in which the student had failed was not to be shown to the students. And after the results were out, the parents of the failing student were called, and the papers were only shown at that time.

As per the rule, my parents were also called, but I didn't inform them. As the time passed, I was getting nervous, tense, and fearful because today I would have to show the results. For me, it was impossible, but I have to make it possible; otherwise, my dad would kick me out. After coming out of the class, I met Sumant.

'How much did you get in history?' I asked.

'Don't ask. It's the worst. I secured only 23 out of 100.'

'What?'

'Yeah, I even don't want to go home. I don't know what my father will do after seeing the marks.'

'Yah. I was also thinking that only our parents have been called, and after getting complaints about us, they will burst like anything.'

'Oh shit! I forgot to ask. How much did you get in maths?'

'It's 48.'

'Oh, just 2 marks less. Otherwise, you could have crossed the boundary line.'

'I have two plans.'

'Plans? What kind?'

'Firstly, we will have to flatter our parents and tell them that in the new school, we are going to rock there by bringing in good marks. And the second one is more crucial. Listen to it carefully. Our parents have been called, and they will be shown our answer sheets. If our parents don't come, then the school will not allow us to sit for the next academic session. But as we are leaving the school, there is no problem at all. The results are in our hands only, and we will not tell our parents that they have been called. Now we will only have to show the results to them and have to beg in front of them to forgive us, and we will have to make some promises,' I said.

'Great!'

After reaching home, I saw Dad sitting on my bed with double-handed handshake.

'Arré, beta, aaooaaoo bus tumhara hi intazartha. I have no more patience left. Show me your results. I have been waiting for so long.'

As I gave him my results, Dad's hands came over his mouth after seeing red marks in maths, and he immediately asked me how I flunked in this. I was dumbstruck, and I did not have an answer for this. But then I also gave my best to flatter him by making promises. And at last, he agreed and left me.

The next day, as I woke up, I was very much excited because I had about nearly ten days to enjoy to the fullest because the new session was only going to start on 1 April. I took breakfast and went to play, and I started spending my whole day playing only. I didn't even touch my books for five days and enjoyed myself to the fullest. But as soon as my father came to know that I was enjoying my days without even touching a book for a minute, he immediately called me and wanted to know the reason behind it, and my obvious reason was that the exams were over.

'You fool. You don't know there is an interview with the principal. He may ask you any question. You must be prepared for that, and if you will not be able to give an answer, then there will be a problem in getting admission. And you must remember that the first impression is the last impression. Go and study.'

I was completely shocked by the fact that I will be given an interview and that any question may be asked. It was my habit that, after being given exams, I would forget all those things which I have read as I only read them but never understood them. These two facts made me freak out.

The next day, I met Sumant and told him about the interview, and from that day, we regained our determination towards studies and started working hard. On 1 April, as we reached Sodepur, there we saw a tall five-floor building.

Dad told me that it was going to be our new school. I was impressed by the infrastructure. As we reached near the school, I saw a big board which was hung on the second floor; written on it in bold and capital letters was 'St Xavier's Institution'.

And also there were three big gates and one small gate beside the first gate. We entered from the small gate, and I saw many buses which were parked and a big playground; behind the playground, there was a park, along with a cave that looked extraordinary.

We went to the third floor as per instructions. I saw a sign outside the office; on it was written 'Senior School Principal Dipti Maheshwari'. I was glad to know that our principal was a lady teacher because ladies were mostly soft-hearted, and therefore, I thought I would have very little chance of getting punishments. But moreover, I was a little bit tense also by just thinking about the type of question I would be asked. Will it be from a syllabus or just a GK question? Will I be able to impress her or not? A lot of questions started running in my mind. At first Dad and I entered the office, and as I entered, I saw many shields and trophies kept behind the principal's chair. A good smile was on the principal's face.

'A very good morning, ma'am.'

'Very good morning. What's your name, and from where are you?'

'Ma'am, my name is Akash Nahata from Sainthia.'

'In which class are you getting admission here, and what was your percentage in your previous class?'

'Ma'am, in eleventh class, and my previous year's percentage was 80.'

'Nice. That means you are a good student. But what's the main purpose behind leaving that school and taking admission here? And which stream are you taking here?'

'Ma'am, actually I am a good cricket player. I have been selected as a district player, and our Ajeet Sir wants me to read in an English-medium school because he thinks that a player must have a good command of English. That's why I am here. And I am taking commerce.'

'Oh, nice. That means you are a good player. Okay, take care. Goodbye. You will get a letter at your home.'

'Have a good day, ma'am.'

'Thank you.'

We came out of the office, and Sumant and his dad entered the office. After ten minutes, they also came out with smiles on their faces. I immediately asked Sumant what happened. He told me that she asked very easy questions, and all the questions were the same as mine.

After a day, we got letters that we had been admitted into the school and that on 5 April we have to join the class. After receiving this news, we all were blissful and decided to get the uniform and the books on the same particular day. In the evening, Sumant and I and our parents went to the Readymade Centre of Sodepur to buy the school uniforms. As we saw the uniforms, Sumant and I were totally shocked because it was the same as the one worn by the lad whom we used to see in the bus while going to school.

After buying the books, we ate some dessert in Madanmohan Misthan Bhandar, which was near to the book house and then came back to our homes.

The First Day

I woke up immediately in the morning, full of determination to work hard from the very first day of the new session in the new school. I was even excited too because today I was going to wear the new uniform, which was the same as the one that lad wore and looked smart in. I immediately took a bath and wore the new uniform with a tie on my neck for the first time. After wearing the new uniform, I went to see myself in the mirror. I looked smarter, more handsome, and more innocent than the guy whom I used to see. I used to say that he looked very smart.

I took breakfast, touched the feet of my parents, and then I went to school. The bus came, and as we went inside the bus, the same lad was there and in same school uniform. He started staring with wide eyes after seeing us in the same uniform. But we were feeling proud because our dream to dress up in the style similar to his came true. Now we also seemed to be like a part of a royal family. As the bus stopped near Sodepur, Panihati, Sumant and I and that lad came down and went to school.

Fortunately, he was in my class also, and his name was Rishabh. I came to know it when the class teacher called his name at the time of taking attendance. After taking attendance, the teacher called all the new students to queue in front of her so that she could write the name of the new students in the class register. As I came to join the queue, a girl was standing in front of me who looked gorgeous.

She was short in height, with brown-and-black hair. She had the most beautiful eyes I had ever seen. Her lips looked as if God had worked with his chisel to make them as perfect and attractive as possible. Even from a distance and with the dim light, I could make out that her cheeks were soft and lovely. All in all, she was literally flawless. Strands of hair kept floating over her beautiful face under the rotating fan. She looked fair with her glowing fair skin. Soft pink lips shone as light fell on them. Simple yet stylish she looked. Her smile was simply gorgeous.

I felt that I was the luckiest person on this planet to witness such beauty. As her chance came, she told the teacher her name and date of birth, which were to be recorded in the school register as per the rule. Her name was Anshika, and her date of birth was 22 May 1996. Her voice was so sweet; it was just like an angel's. After her, it was my turn.

'Ma'am, what's your name? You are just writing our names, but you didn't introduce yourself,' I said.

'Oh, nice question. You made me realize my duties. So, all new students, first of all, I am sorry because I forgot to introduce myself. I am Abhira Dey, your class teacher. I used to teach Hindi as well as history. But in this class, I will teach Hindi. So now are you happy? I hope now you can introduce yourself.'

'Yah, ma'am. Why not? I am Master Akash Nahata from Sainthia, and my DOB is 25 October 1996.'

As I came back to my seat, everybody started gazing at me because of the way I behaved and introduced myself, which was different from everyone. As I took my seat, I heard some of the guys talking about Anshika, who was just sitting behind me. One of them was saying that she looked very hot; the other was saying, 'Don't say something like that. She is your *bhabhi*.' Another was one more daydreamer; he wanted to make her his spouse. I did not know their names, but suddenly I heard it.

'Himanshu, can you imagine her body stats?'

I was stunned to hear this. But suddenly, Abhira Ma'am stood up and started telling us our roll numbers after arranging our names alphabetically. Mine was 7, and Anshika's was 8. I was glad to know that she was after me because I believe that girls are always good in studies, and therefore, she could help me at times of examinations.

The first four periods were on Hindi, history, maths, and English, which passed very smoothly and nicely. The teachers came and interacted with us and went away just because it was the first day. After four periods, it was a recess of thirty minutes. In this period, I enjoyed a lot because it was the first time I saw in a school that every lad and damsel played together; even some friends were sharing their tiffins and eating together. It seems that bonds between friendships were very good.

During recess, I interacted with some new friends—Ananya, Akansha, Anshika, Abhishek, Anuj, and others. Then I told them about myself, that I was a good player, that I was going to play for the district tournament, that I was reading there as per the wish of Ajeet Sir, and that even his club is taking the expense of my studies. And moreover, I made it clear that I was playing for that club, and that was why. They were very happy after knowing this. As the bell rang, all entered their respective classes, and only the prefects were seen outside the classrooms; their duties were to keep the classes silent until the teachers for the fifth period came.

The last three periods were on geography, physics, and chemistry, which also passed very nicely; we only introduced ourselves to the teachers. As the bell rang after the seventh period, all started coming out of their classes for going back to their homes, but I was having little bits of doubts about the subjects. I immediately met Rishabh, who was the only old student whom I know.

He told me there were a total of six subjects: economics, commerce, accounts, English, Hindi, and business math or computer as optional subjects. I started staring at him with wide eyes after hearing that there were a total of six subjects which I have to read here. In my previous school, there were only five subjects, and I failed in mathematics.

'It's common. Now that you are in ISC board, you have to study. And remember one more thing, the ISC board is tougher than any other board,' Rishabh said.

After listening to this, I totally fainted. As I woke up, Rishabh's first question was on what actually happened to me.

'You made me totally fearful.'

I had a simple answer, that I never studied these much subjects. He smiled at my silly answer, and then we went together to our homes. As I stepped inside my home, I saw Dad and Mom were sipping tea on the bed and were eagerly waiting for me. I immediately saw the time; it was 5.40 p.m. I greeted them and told them that I was on time. The school ended at 5.05 p.m., and then I had to walk a mile to catch the bus, so then coming home at 5.40 was normal.

'Did I say anything to you that you are late? I am just waiting here to know how the first day in your new school was,' Dad said.

'Dad, don't ask. It was mind-blowing, excellent, and awesome.'

'Why? What happened that was so good?'

'Dad, the teachers are very good. They interacted with us very nicely. It seems to be like that they are friends and they are even ready to help us at any time for anything. They only want that we behave in a proper and disciplined way in the class, and they even told us that if they find any fault, destruction, or nonsense created by any student, then to them they will behave in a very rude way. They will give strict punishments also. And, Dad, friends are also very good. It is my first co-education school, where boys and girls both study. There is no difference between them or a mindset that they are girls and we are boys. They are all used to study together. And, Dad, I even saw there were groups of friends in which both boys and girls were there. They were just eating their tiffins and sharing with one another. The bond between them was very good. And even today, I have made some new friends, Dad.'

'Oh, that's great. I hope you like that school.'

'Yah, Dad. I like it very much.'

Second Day

Tttrrrrrnnnnggg . . .

The alarm rang at six o'clock, and I woke up immediately full of determination and enthusiasm just because today was the second day—although in actual manner, it was the first day. Yesterday's class was just an interaction between teachers and students, but today teachers were going to teach us. I was getting bored because I had four hours in my hands and I couldn't imagine how to pass the time. In the previous school, the classes started at six thirty in the morning, and I could easily pass the time in the morning. But in Xavier's, the school time is 12 p.m. to 5.05 p.m.

However, I managed to pass the time, and at ten thirty, I dressed up and came out of the home to ride the bus. At eleven fifteen, I had reached the school, and by eleven thirty, the gate closed. After that, no one was allowed to enter the school except the school bus. At eleven thirty sharp, the bell rang, and the students started coming out of the class to make the queue for assembly. It was my first assembly. I did not know where to stand and what to do, but my friends told me that we had to stand just outside the classrooms, in the corridor.

A long queue was there in the corridor on the right side. The girls were standing just beside the casements, and the lads were standing on the left side beside the wall of the classrooms. At eleven forty-five sharp, the assembly started, and sound came from the small speakers, which were hung above the doors of every classroom.

A command was given, 'Assembly Attention', and then the pledge started. After the pledge, all were in the rest position, and news was being announced and, at last, the national anthem. At twelve sharp, the bell rang, and the first period was on mathematics, which was to be taught by Alolika Ma'am. As she entered the class, we greeted her, and in a very good manner, she taught us maths which was easily understood.

The next three periods also went very nicely. At two thirty sharp, the bell rang, and the recess started. At recess, Sumant and I and some other friends were eating tiffins and sharing with one another. Suddenly, Anshika came and joined us.

First Conversation and Punishment

'Hi, guys. I'm Anshika.' She shook hands with each one of us and said, 'Don't feel shy. Eat my tiffin. I also want to be in your group.'

I ate her paratha, and it was awesome.

'Anshika, who made these?' I asked.

'Why?'

'It's dainty.'

'My mom had cooked it.'

'Wow! Tell her to cook every day for you, and I will eat your tiffin each day.'

'Ohh, and what will I eat? It's better if you can eat your own tiffin.'

'Not at all.'

'Hmm, I can share it or give it to you, but not every day. It depends on my mood only.'

'Okay.'

After a heavy and dainty lunch, I was feeling sleepy, but then I also had to attend the remaining three periods. As the fifth period began, it was on history, which was one of the monotonous periods. As Debojita Ma'am started teaching, I started sleeping in the class with my head up facing the board and supported by my palm so that no one would even think that I was sleeping while sitting. But my luck was not good, and Debojita Ma'am caught me while sleeping.

'Rishabh, who is this fellow sleeping in the class? Wake him up,' Debojita Ma'am cried.

'Ma'am, a new student, his name is Akash.'

'Akash,' Debojita Ma'am shouted, and my dream was broken. I panicked.

'Yes, ma'am.'

'Is this a sleeping class or your home?'

'Ma'am, you are wrong. Both the options are invalid. You can give two more options, ma'am, because an MCQ must have four options. After that, I can give you an answer.'

'You nonsense, get lost from my class.'

'It's not possible. A lad five feet and five inches in height, how can he get lost in this small class? If I hide myself, even a bird can see me while flying.'

'You come here. I said come here. I am not joking with you. I said get out of my class.'

'But why?'

'You are asking me? Why, don't you know what you have done? First, sleeping in the class, then arguing with me.'

'I was not sleeping. I was just thinking.'

'Oh, you were thinking by closing your eyes?'

'Yah, ma'am, so that you cannot divert my mind.'

'What the hell are you saying? If I am diverting your mind, it means you are no more interested in the history class.'

'From the first day, I was not interested in knowing about the ancient times and what the kings have done or learning the dates of the wars. They can be seen when required by turning the pages only.'

'Oh, so harsh you are. Can I know what you want to learn and what you were thinking?'

'I want to learn facts and the reason for each and every thing, which will help me in the future, or environmental studies, through which we can learn about the environment.'

'Oh . . . and what were you thinking?'

'I was thinking just how girls b—'

'What did you say? How girls . . . ?'

'Hmm, how girls' brains could work so fast.'

'Hmm. It's enough. Go and kneel down outside the class. And ha, don't enter my class for a week. You will have to be there, and after that, if you want to come into my class, then you will have to ask permission from the principal. Get out.'

After coming out of the classroom, I was extremely happy because now I was free to do anything. Beside our classroom, there was a washroom, and I went there. As the bell rang, I came out of the washroom and sat in a kneeling position outside the classroom. Debojita Ma'am came out, saw me, and went away.

For the next three days, in the same way I passed the history period in the washroom. But on the fourth day, my fate was not good. In between the period, Debojita Ma'am had a call and had to receive it. She came outside the class, and I was not there. She was shocked, and she sent Rishabh in search of me. Rishabh came into the washroom and told me that Debojita Ma'am was calling me. I got scared and came with Rishabh to meet her.

'Ma'am, did you call me?'

'You bloody. What did I say to you?'

'Ma'am, to be in a kneeling position outside the classroom.'

'And where were you? Roaming here and there.'

A nice slap was given to me, and a new punishment was to be a *murga* in the class only. This was the most difficult and disgraceful punishment for me because it was to be done inside the class and in front of the girls. As the period ended, I was not able to show my countenance just because of ignominy. The first reason was the slap, and the second was the murga inside the class. I was just crying from the inside, only the tears were not visualized. As the school ended, I came home alone because of ignominy. And it was one of the nastiest days in my school life.

First Match in SXI

As I reached school, everybody was in search of me because there was a cricket match.

'Thank God you both have come,' my friends said.

'Why?' I asked.

'Today after recess, there is a cricket match between two sections. And each and every member of the school is going to witness the match. There are prizes also, which will be given to the winning team and the man of the match,' my friends said.

Oh, that's good. Today I had a chance to prove my existence in this school by showing my smartness in cricket. After the assembly, the bell rang, and the first period began. It was on mathematics, but Alolika Ma'am didn't come, and we decided the members of the team and set the fielder position in the grounds. After the fourth period, the recess began. We took our lunch, and then we were ready to play the match. All classes started proceeding towards the grounds, taking their respective seats, and even all teachers came to watch the match.

It seemed like that there was a match between India and Pakistan. Our game teacher, Manmohan Sir, was the umpire, and the coin was tossed by the principal. I was the captain of my team, and Rahul was the captain of another team. I chose heads and won the toss. I decided to bat first.

Our team started batting. Rishabh and Abhishek were the openers. They played well the first five overs, and our first wicket fell at 45 runs. Rishabh was out for 25 runs. The second wicket fell at 60 runs on the seventh over, and Piyush was out at 30 runs. After twelve overs, the score was 90 for 3.

Sumant came on the strike. I believed that he could send the score of our team up to 100 within three overs. The first ball hit by Sumant was a massive six over the head of the umpire, then a four, six, and again, a four. In the first over, he secured 20 runs, and on 11.4 overs, the score reached 100 runs. On the fifteenth over, one more wicket fell, and our scoreboard read 120 for 4.

I came on the grounds, and Sumant was on the strike. He hit the ball on the back side, and we took a run. Then I was on the strike. The first ball I hit was a four, and not only this, all balls in this over were fours. After the sixteenth over, the scoreboard read 144, and after the twentieth over, the score read 200 for 4 wickets. I secured 70 runs by taking 10 singles, 12 fours, and 2 sixes. And Sumant secured 75 runs by taking 17 singles, 10 fours, and 3 sixes. And finally, we reached a winning score of 200 runs in our quota of twenty overs, and the opposition needed 201 runs to win in their twenty overs.

I started proceeding with the first ball. I bowled a perfect yorker that Aamir placed away with ease. The next two balls were dots. My fourth yorker ball threw the middle stump, and Aamir was clean bowled. After the first over, the score was 6 for 1 wicket. Sumant took the ball for the second over, and he bowled a decent over for the batsman, but took 1 wicket. The score reached 18 for 2 in the second over.

I again came to the ball, but Raj made a mockery of my fastest bowling and proved me wrong. He hit four consecutive fours on my ball. On the fifth ball, I bowled him with a yorker, and on the sixth, I took another wicket. After the end of the three overs, the score read 25 for 4.

The opponent batted wisely. They took singles and doubles for the next eighteen overs, and the score reached 180 for 8 in thirteen overs. It seems like that match can be won by any team, and our total even looked small. Sumant bowled a good over and gave only 4 runs with a wicket in the same over.

The match reached the final over. The scorecard read 184 for 9 in nineteen overs. They needed 17 runs in six balls with a wicket in hand. Game could have gone anywhere until I bowled a last over with full determination.

I took the ball for the last over. I was confident. For the first ball of the twentieth over, the batsman drove the ball to the cover, and it was a four. For the second ball, the batsman came out of the crease and drove the ball over the head of the umpire for a six. Suddenly, the match seemed to be slipping from our hands. I threw the third ball in a swinging yorker, which helped me uproot the middle stump of the batsman. And finally, we won the match by 7 runs.

The supporters and the classmates of our team came on the crease and started hugging and praising us for the nice game played by our team. After playing the fabulous game, we came back to our seats. Beside us, all the girls were there; they started praising us.

But I was in search of Anshika. I saw her, and she passed a smile and greeted me, 'Nicely played.'

I became more excited as she greeted me because she was my first female friend, and I want to talk and spend more time with her. And on that day, whenever she passed me a smile or talked to me on her own, I would become happier.

Soon, after fifteen minutes, prize distribution started, and everyone started gathering near the stage. The principal was there to give away the prizes. Firstly, the runner-up's team was called, and a medal was given to every player. Then the captain of the runner-up team was called and was asked to share something.

'Good evening, guys. I am feeling very happy to be a runner-up because we learn from our mistakes only. And I am feeling proud to say that our opponent team has defeated us. And I am ready to learn cricket from our opponent team only because in learning no one is smaller or bigger. The person who has knowledge is always bigger, and there is no shame to learn from our friends also. Thank you,' Rahul said.

After that, the winning team was called, and each member was given a 500-rupee cash award.

'And now, the most awaited result. Man of the Match goes to—I know, students, you are very much in suspense to know. Can anyone guess it?

Suddenly, there was a pause throughout the whole grounds, which earlier had been filled with shouting like anything. Now everyone stood silent, and we the players started staring at one another's faces with the curiosity of knowing who the hero of today's match was.

'It goes to none other than Akash!'

After hearing this, my chest was puffed up just because I was selected as the man of the match. As I came on the stage, everybody started shouting and hooting for me. Dipti Ma'am handed me the Man of the Match trophy and a cheque of 5,000 rupees. I was too excited after getting a cheque just because I got another chance to give a surprise to my dad. As

I came down from the stage, Anshika greeted me by saying, 'Keep it up,' and she even shook a hand with me. It was so soft, and it seemed like I have touched cotton.

'Goodbye. See you tomorrow. And ha, start preparing for our first evaluation examination. It's going to start,' she said.

'Oh please, you know that I don't want to study. When you are there, why worry about an exam?'

'Oh, mister, please don't be dependent upon me. Nobody knows about tomorrow. It may happen that the seating arrangements may change.'

'Please don't be so pessimistic. Be optimistic.'

'Okay, babaa. Goodbye.'

'Goodbye, and have a good day,' I said.

As she went away, I met Sumant and came back home along with him. Mom and Dad were sipping tea when I entered the home. At that time, I handed the cheque to my father. After handing over the cheque, Dad became very excited, and again he hugged me and praised me.

First Evaluation

The next day, I reached school and saw a group of students gathering near the notice board. I understood that there must be some new notice. I saw the notice board. It was the date sheet for the first evaluation, and it was going to start on the week after. As I saw it, I felt like I was going to faint just because for me one week was a very short time to prepare. But then I also met Anshika and asked her to help me in the examination time. She was not ready to help, but she relented.

The first paper was for English I, and on this subject, I was weak because it was full of the grammar portion. On the week of the examination, every day I came full of preparation, but I came full of preparation for cheating with Anshika's help. The class teacher came and made a queue roll-numbers-wise. Anshika's roll number was 8, and mine was 7. The teacher instructed us to sit with four students on a single bench. After hearing this, I became more excited because four students sitting on a single bench made it easier for me to cheat, and secondly, I got a chance to sit with Anshika, which I had wanted for many days.

As I took my seat beside the Anshika, I started gossiping with her, and she also even started sharing how she had prepared for the examination. As the whole class took their respective seats, the teacher announced that till the examination is over, we all had to be seated only in this way. This info made me happier because I got the chance to sit with Anshika for all seven periods till the examinations are over.

The fifth period was our examination for English. Debojita Ma'am came and distributed the question papers. After seeing the questions, my mind stopped working, and I became dependent upon Anshika only. After she started writing the answers, only then did I start copying from her. After twenty-five minutes, she completed her paper and kept her paper in a vertical position so that I could cheat more easily. After thirty minutes, I also completed my paper. The bell rang after forty minutes, and Debojita Ma'am took away the papers and went out.

'Thank you very much. If you had not been there, then I would have flunked,' I said.

'Please, Akash, we are good friends. Don't talk like that. I am always here to help you.'

'Let's ask our other friends about their exams. Hey, Anshika, Akansha is going. Call her,' I said.

'You call her. Your voice is louder than mine.'

'Akansha!' I shouted.

'Yes.'

'Wait. How was your exam?'

'Nice. What about you both?'

'Mine was awesome. You know, when Anshika is there beside me, my exam will always be nice because I always cheat with her help.'

'But did you ever think what would happen if she stops showing you her anwers?'

'Nothing will happen at that time. I will start working hard on my own.'

'Oh, that's great. Then why don't you work hard from now on? It will help only you, not anyone else.'

'Oh please, I work only when my mind says so.'

'Okay, leave this entire thing. Are you ready to play truth, dare or situation? This period is free,' she said.

'Who said it is free?'

'I'm saying, na? It's free. Are you willing to play or not?'

'Yes, why not?' Anshika and I said.

'Then let's go to the last bench and ask others also if they want to play with us. I'll be back in a minute.'

By the time Akansha was back. I had called our whole group.

'Okay, guys, the rules—I hope that you all know it. Nevertheless, let me repeat it. The pen will be rotated, and whoever the tip of the pen faces will be asked a question by the person facing the back side of the pen. Let's start.'

Sumant rotated the pen.

And the opener was Rishabh.

'Yes, what do you choose?'

'Truth,' he said with a sheepish grin.

'Hmm, well then, let me think.'

And in a second, Akansha blurted out the question. It was clear that she had it prepared in her mind.

'Well, if you get a chance for a one-night stand, with whom will you want to do it with?'

He said that he would go out with Tanya, a girl from our class. She actually behaved like she wanted to get laid.

I said, 'Bhai, you don't have to even think. Just tell her, she will agree to it.'

Next, Rishabh got the chance to ask a question to Anshika.

'Yah, Anshika, what do you want? Truth, dare, or situation?'

'Dare.'

'Okay. Your dare is you have to crack a joke.'

'Okay. Hmm . . . yes. Once upon a time, there were two friends who went for an interview. One was talented, and the other was foolish. At first, the talented one entered the room, and he was asked who the PM of the nation was. He said, "Manmohan Singh." The second question was "Where should we throw the trash?" He replied, "In the dustbin." The third question was "How many stars are there, boy?" He replied, "It is not known. Till date, scientists are working on it." After this, he was told to go back. As he came out, the foolish boy asked him what was asked. The talented boy replied to him, "Whatever will be asked, say 'Manmohan Singh' as the answer to the first question, 'dustbin' to the second one, and 'It is not known, scientists are working on it' to the third one." As the foolish one entered the room, he was asked what his name was. He replied, "Manmohan Singh." For the second question, he was asked where he used to live. He replied, "Dustbin." And for the third question, he was asked the name of his father, and he said that it was not known and that scientists were working on it.'

A huge laugh broke out among us. Again, Sumant rotated the pen, and he himself got a chance to ask a question to Akansha.

'So, Akansha, what do you want?' Sumant said.

'Dare.'

'Oh, that's great. I hope you remember that you told us in the beginning that non-vegs are allowed. Am I correct?'

'Yah.'

'Okay then. I am giving you a very easy dare because you started this. So the dare is you have to seduce any guy in our class.'

'What? Okay, I will do it.' She got up and started thinking about whom to have a go on. She finally picked up Sumant.

She went near him, walking like a model. She started moving around him speaking or, I must say, murmuring some words like *hot* or that's what I heard.

A huge laugh broke among us, and we continued laughing for a long time. She had done her dare really well.

'Okay, guys, let's continue it,' I said. I rotated the pen.

'Yes, now Anshika will ask Akash,' Ananya said.

'So, Akash, what do you want?'

'Truth.'

'Okay then. Your question is "If you get a chance to visit Paris, then which girl will you choose from our class to go along with you?"'

'Okay, if I will say the truth, then promise me no one will be angry with me because, first of all, I am timid and, second, I am feeling fearful to say.'

'Okay, promise.'

'It's you only, Anshika.'

'What?'

'Yes.'

As I said a yes, I saw a smile and a bashful look on her countenance, which made me feel like I saw adoration for me in her eyes. I too became happy after seeing her chuckle.

After I rotated the pen, the chance came for Akansha to ask a question to Rishabh. Rishabh chose a dare, and he was dared to say a non-veg joke in a loud voice so that everyone could hear it.

'What the hell are you saying? I can't say a joke in front of the class because if I will say the joke which I know at present, then the girls will start beating me with their shoes. I can say it here only, Akansha, please.'

'No, you can't.'

'See, Sumant and I told Anshika and you to crack a joke in front of us only. We didn't tell you to share to the class. But why are you doing this? You know there are some girls who are very innocent and may complain to the teacher because they are complain box. You know that.'

'Yah, I know that. That's why I am saying it. I am no fool like you both that I will give a dare so easy. You gave us dares to say the joke here only. That was your fault, not mine. And ha, before you decided to take a dare, you should have thought about it many times because as you should know, the person who is going to give you a dare is Akansha, not a simple girl.'

'What?'

'Yah.'

'Akansha, please. I am folding my hands in front of you. Please forgive me. Please change the dare.'

'Okay, if you are requesting me so much, then I am changing the dare.'

'Thank you very much.'

'Hmm . . . Yah, a new dare for you. Approach the girl whom you think is innocent and who may complain to the teacher. Go and slap her or propose to her—anyone. I am giving you three options now.'

'What the hell are you saying? Would you like to kill me or what?'

'I don't know. Now you have altogether three options—joke, slap, or propose to anyone. You can do it, and ha, I can't wait for you any more. I will count up to ten, and within ten seconds, be prepared to do any one of them. Otherwise, be ready for punishment of sixty sit-ups while holding your ears after school and even outside the main gate in between the roads and obviously in front of everyone.'

'Imagine it. What are you saying? There was not such a rule said in the beginning of the game.'

'Why should it be said? It is common. When we took admission into the school, the principal didn't tell us that if we fail to do homework, disturb the class, or create nonsense, then they will give us punishment. This was also not said, but it is common.'

'Oh. You are really great. No one can fight with you. I'm ready to do the first one only.'

'Yah, good. But ha, first you have to make the class silent, and then you have to crack the joke because everyone is busy talking.'

'Okay. Yes, guys, listen carefully. There is an announcement.'

And everybody stayed silent.

'I am sorry. There is no announcement. Actually I have got a dare to crack a joke. So please listen and forgive me. Ek bar pappu apne balcony mai nanga sarir khada tha to raste se guzarte uske dost ne bola pappu tera sina to bada mast hai yaar. Aree Ya to kuch bhi nahi tu apne bhabhi ka dekhega to tu behosh ho jayega.'

As he finished the joke, each girl started staring at him in such a manner that it seems like they were going to kill him. And as he was thinking this, suddenly a girl came out of her seat with a ruler in her hand. He got fearful and shouted, 'Akansha, help me!' And he was saved by Akansha.

The next few days, we had the exams, and I cleared them easily with the help of Anshika. On the last day of the exams, Anshika and I were sitting together, and on the sixth period, we were having the exam. On the third period, I was shocked to see Anshika because as I turned my head backwards, I saw her panties, which had a white background and a pink teddy printed on it. I saw it on the side of the skirt where the pockets used to be and above which the skirt was hooked.

I started grinning. Firstly, I was afraid to watch it again and again because if she caught me, then I would be in hell. Secondly, I thought of telling her because if any other guy would see it, he may also start grinning, and her dignity would be lost. But I had no guts to say that. But then I also flattered her first.

'Anshika, can I say something?'

'What?'

'At first, say you will not be angry and that you will not break our friendship also.'

'Okay, babaa. I will not break our friendship. Say it.'

'Nah. Nah. Sorry. I am feeling fearful in saying it to you.'

'Oh please. I will not say anything to you.'

'Your skirt is torn. Get it stitched. Your panties are visible.'

'What? Oh, thank you.'

She stood there, immediately adjusted her pocket, sat down, and asked me to see whether it's okay or not. I was feeling ignominious seeing it again, but she was feeling no shame saying to me to check it out, whether it was fine or not. I didn't look back at that place, but she continued talking and started saying to me that it was not torn, that the girls' skirts were like that, and that actually the pocket only moved away and that was why her panties were seen.

'Are you angry with me for whatever I have said to you?'

'No. Not at all. You are sitting beside me. You saw, and you told me. That's a good job done by you. It might happen that if any other guy had seen, they would have simply made fun of me.'

The sixth period began. Debojita Ma'am came and distributed the papers for mathematics. The paper was very easy because for the first time, I came full of preparation, and I even finished the paper before the time. My exams went well. After the exams, as school ended, Sumant and I went home together in a jolly mood because our exams went well.

'Hi. I want to ask you one thing.'

'What?' Sumant asked.

'Not here. Meet me in a deserted place.'

'Why?'

'It's personal.'

'Okay then. Come to the grounds as soon as possible after changing your clothes.'

When I reached home, the time was 5.30 p.m. I quickly changed and went to the grounds. Sumant was already there, waiting for me. As I approached him, he immediately asked me what the matter was.

'It's a serious matter. Please tell me what love is.'

'Love? Why are you asking me this thing?'

'You just tell me.'

'Listen. Till today, I hadn't loved any girl. Till date, I don't even think of love. And I do not even have any experience of having love for any girl, so I cannot explain it to you. But ha, I can say at least that love is something through which a person can feel pain and happiness with another person without telling each other. But please tell me the reason behind asking me this question.'

'The problem is that nowadays I am not getting any interest for academics. Whenever I sit for a self-study, after reading two or three lines, I would get an image of Anshika in my brain, and I start thinking of her only.'

'So what's wrong in thinking about her? You both are good friends. You may think about her.'

'But, Sumant, the problem is that I am thinking more and more about her only. It seems that we are not only good friends. Instead, she is a very close friend of mine. And you know what? I used to think that her roll number should always only be after my roll number so that I can sit with her my whole life. I want to take the same stream as her after tenth, whichever she will take. I want to work hard in the twelve classes also so that I can attain good marks like her and I could get admitted into the same college as her. I even want to spend all my money on her in my college life by taking her to movies, cafes, etc. And I even have made plans for marriage. In our family, there's a rule that we have to marry a girl of the same caste, but as she is Bengali, I have made plans for that also. I will set a priest to whom I will give money without telling my parents, and he will make our marriage like an arranged marriage. Then I will marry her, and after spending years together, when we will be having a child at that time, Anshika and I will tell the truth to our parents, that we were friends from our school life, that the priest had told a lie at the time of our wedding, that she is Bengali, and all blah and blah.'

'Akash, you are great. You have thought a lot about her. I will say only one thing. If you both are really good or close friends and if you are thinking so much about her with the way you have made future plans and the way you are ready to give your life as per her wishes, then you just go and propose to her. I think this can only be love.'

'But, Sumant, I am getting second thoughts also in my mind. Love is something which happens between parents and children or between spouses. Take this as an example. Suppose anything happens to us, our parents would become tense, and they would pray and cry for us. But if something happens to you, at that time I will be upset also, but not as much as your parents would be. I want to say that the way we love our parents is not the same way as I love Anshika. Then how can I say that I am in love with her?'

'Yah, you are right. That's why I am saying you propose to her. If she accepts it, then you will love her will in the same way that you love your parents. Also, you love her now, but it is one-sided. When the love is from both sides, then it increases very much.'

'Yah, I think you are right. I love Anshika. But I think I don't have the guts to say it to her.'

'But you have to say it. Otherwise, someone else will take her from your heart, and you will keep on watching.'

'No, it will never happen. Tomorrow, I am going to tell her about this.'

First Trial

The next day as I woke up, I was very happy because I was going to propose to her, but I was also feeling fearful to say it to her. Contrary to my daily routine, today I took a bath for a long time. It took me thirty minutes to take a bath. After that, I dressed immediately, but again, setting my hair took me fifteen minutes. This was the longest time I had ever taken to get ready for school. But why not? Today was a special day for me.

As I reached the school, I saw Anshika and Akansha talking with each other. I passed her a smile, and she also passed it back. Then the recess began.

I thought, *Akash, today you have to say that you love her. But should I say it today only, or should I talk with Anshika for some more days so that our friendship will become stronger? But she is with a group of girls. How can I say it to her? Say something. Otherwise, you will not get a chance to say it again after recess. I am going to call her.*

I said, 'Hi, Anshika. How are you?'

'I'm fine. What about you?'

'Me too. Fine.'

'I will talk with you later. Bye-bye,' she said.

After the recess, the fifth period was English. Ratna Ma'am would take the class. She came in.

'Students, please be quiet. This class is a really very disturbing class. All stupid creatures are here. Give me a ruler.'

I thought, *Every day she would come and shout like anything to us, and if anybody gave her a ruler, then like anything she would bang it on the table. And then if she saw anyone disturbing the class, then she would beat him like a dog. Today make fun of her, Akash. But, Akash, she will start beating you only. No problem. If you have the guts, then do it, and from only here will you gain the guts to say to Anshika that you love her. Do it. Do it.*

I said, 'Ma'am, I have a ruler. Wait.'

'Yah, give it to me first.'

'Yah, ma'am. Take it.'

'You bloody fool. What the hell are you doing? Am I joking here in the class?'

'No, ma'am.'

'Then what is this?'

'A ruler.'

'Did I ask for this ruler?'

'I don't know, ma'am. You didn't mention what kind of ruler you required in the beginning, whether you needed a big, small, wooden, plastic, or steel ruler. Then how will I be able to know what you need. You just told us you need a scale. I have the small plastic scale. That's why I gave it to you. And now you are shouting at me. It's not fair.'

'You stupid nonsense. Are you a new student, or do you not know that I need a big scale every day? I used to say that, and anyone from you all would only give me a big scale. Were you sleeping on all those days?'

'But, ma'am, if you require it each day, then why don't you buy it?'

'What? Ya give me that scale,' she said.

Chat! Chat!

'Ah! Ah! Why are you beating me?'

'Get lost from this class.'

After school, as I came back, I realized that my special day had become the worst day. The next day, as I went to school, I had a plan to meet Anshika and say to her that I was going for the district team. As the recess began, I met her.

'Hi, Anshika, I have good news.'

'Good news? Say it to me first. Many days have passed, and I haven't listened to any good news.'

'I don't think it will be good news for you, but it's good for me.'

'Yah? Then tell me also. You are my good friend. If you will be happy, then I will also be happy.'

'Really? Okay. The news is that—you know that I am a good player in cricket, so tomorrow I am going to play for the district team. If I play good there, then I will be selected for a state team.'

'Wow! That's awesome news. Work hard. I know you can do it. Best of luck.'

She moved her hand to shake mine. I touched her palm and shook her hand. Her hand was soft as teddy and as sweet as candy. She had a voice that jingled like a Christmas bell; she was as warm as a sweater.

'Thank you. Now I think I can play better because now you are a supporter of mine.'

'No, I am not a supporter. I'm your friend. When you go for the district team, I will miss you a lot, and I will even pray to God for you so that you can get selected for the state.'

'Oh. That's nice. I will miss you too.'

After school, I realized that it was one of my fabulous days, just the opposite of the previous day. I started thinking of Anshika and the way she forwarded her hand to shake mine. As I touched her palm, the softness of her hand as well as her heart made me feel a sense of love towards her, which was forcing me to hug her, but I couldn't. The way she said that she would miss me and would pray to God for me, it seemed that she also loved me. But only God knows the truth. Instead of 'I will miss you too', I was going to reply 'I love you', but I couldn't.

After two days, as I came back to school, I met Anshika.

'Hi, Anshika. Hi.'

'Hi. When did you come back, and how was your match?'

'I only came back yesterday night, and the good news is that I have been selected for the state team also.'

'What? So nice you are. I said, na, you will get selected if you will play well and work hard. By the way, what about your performance?'

'I secured 110 out of 85 balls and was not even out. I smashed 5 sixes and 10 fours, and I even took 2 wickets. And the best thing is that I was awarded the Man of the Match, for which I got a mobile as a gift and a cheque of 5,000 rupees. And my father also got a promotion.'

'Wow! That's awesome.'

'One more thing is that our beloved friend Sumant was also selected for the state team.'

'Wow!'

'Do you know that my parents are very happy with my performance in cricket? They want the same kind of performance in academics also, but I don't know why I am not able to perform well in academics.'

'Don't worry. You will be able to perform well in academics also. Work hard, and one day you will succeed in it also. I hope you have heard one quote in Hindi: "Kosis karnai walo ki kabhi har nahi hoti aur har maan lene walo ki kabhi jay jaykar nahi hoti.'"

'OMG! You are good in Hindi too? It's good. Do you know? I would give to my parents whatever money I have earned through cricket without spending a little bit of it. They would be blissful because they know that I know the value of money. And do you know one more thing? Today, due to this money and the money which my father had saved through his earnings, it helped us construct a home for us, which is going to be inaugurated within a week.'

'Wow, that's very good! And by the way, what about your mobile?'

'Mobile will be with me only because my father had permitted me to use it.'

The bell rang, and recess was over. We went inside the classroom. After school, I was very blissful after collecting the numbers of my friends because now I also have a mobile. After collecting them, Sumant and I went on the bus for our return home. He asked me whether I was able to get the number of Anshika or not, and my answer was a big no.

'Are you mad or what? You love her, and you didn't take her number?' he said.

'Actually, the problem is that, first of all, I am feeling fearful of asking for her number. The second reason is that if I ask her and if she denies me, then what will be my image? I will only lose my dignity there. And the third is that I have already told her that I have a mobile. I was waiting for her to ask my number.'

'Oh, great person, remember one thing. The girls never ask the number of a boy until and unless it becomes very important for them, and you are thinking that she will ask for your number? It's impossible. You will keep on waiting, but that day will never come. I am advising you, ask for her number tomorrow. Don't get fearful. She will give you her number. She will never deny it because she is your good friend. And don't think so much of your dignity and all these things. Otherwise, you will not be able to propose to her your whole life. And even if you are so aware of your dignity, you didn't think about your family's dignity when you had made plans to marry her in the future by telling a lie to your parents. Did you ever think what will happen if your parents will come to know that you have married a Bengali girl?'

'Really, I haven't thought over this entire thing. You are right. Tomorrow I will take her number,' I said.

'Hi, Anshika. Hi,' I said.

'Hi. How are you?'

'I'm fine. Actually, I forgot to ask one thing yesterday,' I said.

'What?'

'I took everybody's numbers, but I forgot to take your number. May I have your number?' I said abruptly.

'My number? Well, I don't give my number to boys because most of them make wrong use of it. They use it only to disturb me. But as you are asking, I will give it to you because you are a good friend. It's 9836512068, and ha, never call me. You can only SMS me. Akash, write it down now. I will not repeat it again,' she said with a mischievous wink.

I was stunned by that wink. By stunned, I mean really stunned. I stood there like a frozen mummy.

Man, that smile—was I dreaming? Sweetheart, ohh my angel, that wink and that innocent smile after just made me almost fall in love with her all over again.

'Akash?'

'Yah, yah. I will SMS you only, and don't worry, I will remember your number, 9836512068.' I recited the number like a small student who had just learned the alphabet. *Well, all that doesn't matter now because now I only have to propose to her. I love you, angel. I love you.*

'Sumant, I took it. I took it. I took it.' I came running to Sumant.

'What did you take?' he asked with a horrified face.

Ignoring it, I said, 'Obviously, her number.'

And the next thing i know, he was down on his knees, laughing in an uncontrollable manner.

'What are you laughing for?'

'Arré, you came running happily and shouting, "I got it. I got it." What do you think we all made out of it?' And the next moment, all my other buddies also started laughing with him.

I wasn't able to understand what he meant, but I was sure that it was again some of his double-meaning jokes.

'Well done. Be in touch with her through the cell,' he said after he was done with his laugh.

After supper, I quickly typed an SMS to Anshika: 'Each and every event can be seen in two ways—either positive or negative—and our choice will define our destiny. Goodnight.'

After sending this message, I went to bed to sleep. But I couldn't sleep until and unless I could get a reply. After a minute, my cell vibrated, which brought a smile to my face because the notification showed that the message was from Anshika.

I quickly opened the message, and it read: 'So nice you are ☺ ☺!'

After reading this, I became blissful, and the two smiling faces after the message made me smile even more. I was not able to sleep. I was thinking about her only when suddenly I received another message, which read: 'Goodnight.'

Angel's Address

The last message made me doze off well through the whole night.

'What happens if she is angry with you or what?' Sumant said.

'No, yaar, we are interacting with each other very nicely,' I said.

'Then what?'

'I want to meet her. I don't mean meeting her in class. I mean to say that I want to meet her in front of her house. I want to know her address.'

'What?'

'Yah. You just tell me how to get it,' I said.

'But why are you not satisfied with meeting her in class?'

'No, it's nothing like that. I just want to.'

'See, I can say only one thing. I hope you know that . . .'

'What?'

'She goes home in a Sumo.'

'Yah'.

You only have to follow that car to know where she lives. But, Akash, the problem is that nowadays we are coming in a school vehicle, which is fixed by our parents. And what will you tell the driver uncle? Earlier, we used to go alone, but now it's a problem.'

'Yah. I have got an idea,' I said.

'No problem. Go for it. Dar ke aage jeet hai. But at least tell me what you have planned.'

'My plan is that, at first, I have to tell a lie to my parents and have to go with my bicycle, giving any excuse, just before the school time. Then I have to park my cycle in the parking lot which is just near our home. Then I will enter my home without my cycle. Obviously, my mom will ask me about my cycle, and I will tell her that while riding a cycle, my tire burst due to intense heat and I have given that cycle for repairing and by the eve it will get repaired. After that, I have to tell a lie to uncle that today my father will take me to school so he can go. I am coming with my father. When he goes away, then I will take out my cycle from the parking lot, and then I can go to school by riding it. And after school, I can ride my cycle behind her car,' I said.

'Nice plan, Akash, but what about the fact that you will not be able to reach home at the right time?'

'Yah, you are right. I didn't even think of that. But yah, I can do one thing. Every Saturday, there would be half- day classes. But on this Saturday, I will tell Mom that due to the exams which are coming, there will be an extra class for an hour. And on that day only, I will act according to the plan,' I said.

'Oh, you are really great, yaar,' he said.

'But ha, I need your help because it may happen that my mom may ask you about the extra class. You have to just say yes,' I said.

'Okay, it's fine, but what if your mom will come to know that I didn't even go for extra classes then?'

'You do one thing. As you will come back after school, be in your home only. Don't come outside your home unless I come back,' I said.

The Saturday arrived, and I acted according to the plan. I even got successful in fooling my mom and uncle, and I went to school by riding my cycle. And I even submitted the cycle in the school's cycle stand. After the school, I became very much excited to see Anshika's home. But I was a little bit scared also because it was going to be my first ride on a cycle on the main road. But I always knew that 'dar ke aage jit hai'. That's why I dared to go for a ride.

I took my cycle and hid myself behind the house and started peeping for her and her car. And I also wished that Anshika would sit in the middle row of the Sumo so that I could ride my cycle behind her Sumo very easily and she wouldn't even notice me. And it happened as I wanted. As we reached the main road, the Sumo took the speed of nearly about sixty kilometres per hour, which was impossible for me to keep up with while riding a cycle.

But then, I also gave my whole energy to pedalling the cycle. I was able to see only the colour of the Sumo from a long distance, which helped me to follow her. Suddenly, the same Sumo stopped. Anshika came out, and she went away with an old person who was standing there. I saw them from some distance. By the time I reached the point where she had come out, the Sumo went away, and she started walking. I also started following her through walking, and at last, she entered into her home, which was nearly about half a kilometre inside from the main road.

It was a two-storey building; the boundary wall was coloured in cream. The roof had the structure of an aeroplane, which looked marvellous. And on the first floor, there was a balcony, which was at the right place because from there the pond can be seen and the fresh air can enter.

The home was attached to the pond water. I took a long breath and got relaxed because my second task had been completed.

From there, I immediately took a U-turn with my cycle and came back to my home; this took exactly an hour extra to our daily schedule. I changed my clothes and immediately met Sumant and told him the entire incident. He was also happy to know that I succeeded in this plan.

Practical Exam

As I reached school, in the assembly it was announced that there will be a practical test in computer in the first period. I smacked my palm against my forehead just because I was not prepared at all. I was busy all day thinking about her only. But I knew that she will surely help me in the exam, and it was most beneficial for me that her roll number was just after mine. As we entered the class after assembly, I greeted her.

'Hi, Anshika,' I said.

'What?'

'Please help me. Actually, I forgot that there was a test today.'

'Do you ever remember about studies? I can't help you. Sorry. It has been your habit. I don't want to destroy my friend's future,' she said.

'Arré, there's no relation between the practical exam in computer and my future,' I said.

'There is.'

'Please, maan jaoo na. You are so cute,' I said.

'Don't even try to flatter me.'

'And by the way, in the future, I don't want to opt for computer science,' I said.

'So what? This cheating habit is not good,' she said.

'Please be empathic. I hope you know the punishment of Raja Sir. It's very painful. The way he would pull the sideburns of the lads, it's the worst. Even after some time, it would lead to headaches. And I hope you remember that he even warned us that if any one of us would get less than 10 out of 20, then he would give punishments as well as call our guardians. But I know you damsels never get such types of punishments, so how then can you realize the pain? Whenever the teacher would scold you, you girls would start crying, and the teacher would get emotionally blackmailed. There and then only, you avoid getting punished,' I said.

'Okay, babaa. Thik hai. I will show you,' she said.

'Thank you. Thank you very much,' I said.

The bell rang, and we rushed to the computer lab. We sat according to the roll number. She was just beside me, with a distance of a metre. I became more blissful because first of all, I thought that she will be sitting behind me. That's why I flattered her so much. If I had known that she would be sitting beside me, then there would be no problem at all. I can easily see her computer.

Raja Sir came and started distributing the question papers. I was blissful to see the paper because it had only one question to be solved. But then my happiness was shattered into pieces as I came to know that Anshika got another question. The roll numbers 5 and 6, who were sitting in front of me, got another question, and those sitting behind me got another question. It had become very difficult for me to cheat.

'Hi, Anshika. Help me,' I said.

'Copy it,' she said.

'Arré, I have got a different question,' I said.

'What?'

'Yah. See the question paper?' I said.

'You have to wait. Let me finish first. But ha, you can do one thing. Just start copying it except the third, fifth, sixth, and eighth lines because only these lines will be changed. Except for those lines, all are the same,' she said.

'Thanks,' I said.

I started copying it out. She completed her program within fifteen minutes only, and then she started prompting me slowly. I also completed the program with only five minutes left. Raja Sir announced to us as soon as the bell rang: 'You have to minimize the program, and if I caught anyone doing the program or asking anyone, then be ready to get your 5-mark deduction.'

Only two minutes left, and I suddenly saw Anshika sweating like anything even in the AC room. Her eyes were red, and she started crying. I was stunned to see that.

'Hi, Anshika. What happened?' I asked.

'I don't know which button was pressed by me mistakenly, but my whole program has vanished. And I didn't save it also. Raja Sir may or may not believe me that I did the program, but he will also not give me extra time.'

I immediately pressed the Ctrl+Z, and the whole program appeared again on the desktop. The bell rang, and as she looked back to her desktop, the program was there. A smile came over her face. As we came out of the lab, she thanked me a lot.

'Akash, thank you very much today. You have saved me. Otherwise, what would have happened, I don't know. Today you have done a great job. I don't know how to thank you,' she said.

'It's fine, yaar. But I would like to say one thing. When you were crying, you looked like—I don't know what to say.

The tears in your eyes made them sparkle like diamonds. You looked really cute though you were in tears, and trust me, no one can resist helping a sweet girl like you. Well, I can't be sure about others, but trust me, I can't.'

'Aww so sweet of you, and thank you for the compliment. I am really flattered,' she said with a pleasant smile.

Ohh my god, that smile again.

On the way back home, I told this incident to Sumant, and Rishabh also invited us to his birthday party.

'It's the right time to tell her that you love her. Today you have helped her. She is happy with you. Don't miss the chance to say it to her. If you can't say it face to face, then SMS her. But say it to her. You will not get another opportunity like this.'

I realized that Sumant was correct, and as soon as I reached home, I changed my clothes and messaged her.

'Hi, Anshika. What's going on?'

Within thirty seconds, I got a reply. I understood that she was only busy with her mobile. That was why I received a message so fast. 'I'm playing a game in my cell, and coz of you, I am really happy. Thanks a lot.'

I immediately replied to her. 'I want to say one thing to you. Please don't be angry, and promise me that you will not break our friendship.'

And the messaging started.

Anshika: 'I promise.'
Akash: 'I had wanted to say this to you for so many days, but I didn't . . .'
Anshika: 'Yah, tell me.'
Akash: 'I love you.'

I sent it, but I didn't get a response for five minutes. I was feeling reluctant to send another message. Lots of thoughts were coming into my mind. Did I do the right thing? Was I justified? I was over-adventurous, wasn't I? Why did I rush through things? Did I know Anshika well enough? Did she know me well enough? Would she accept what I said? Would she still be my friend? If not, then would we still be on speaking terms? What if she thinks badly of me now? Is our friendship over?

I was worried, anxious, tense, and nervous at the same time. I took my cell from my desk to type another message, but my cell beeped, and I got a message from Anshika. I opened the message.

'Okay. It's fine.'

I didn't understand what she actually meant to say. I immediately replied to her.

'I don't understand what you want to say. Please say it clearly just like the way I said it please.'

After a minute, I got a message.

'I love you too.'

When I read this, I literally started shouting with happiness.

Birthday Party

As I woke up, I remembered that today was Rishabh's birthday, and I was also really happy with the fact that now my love was with me. I wanted to go to his birthday bash, but I knew that I would not get permission from my dad to go because he didn't want that I would miss class. I remembered the day of my aunt's wedding. I requested my dad to let me skip school, but he didn't allow me to. He sent me to school, and he also said that the wedding was going to happen in the evening and that there was no harm in going to school in the daytime, so I had to go to school.

And today was my friend's birthday, and it was impossible to get permission from Dad to miss the class and enjoy the party. But I was very much interested to go to the birthday party. I made plans to bunk off school. And I acted according to the plan. I carried a civil T-shirt in my bag, which my parents did not know. I dressed in my school uniform, took breakfast, and went to school in the school van, which was fixed by my parents.

But as the van dropped me in front of the school gate, I quickly hid myself and went to another street instead of going inside the school. As the place was deserted, I hid myself behind the building and quickly opened my schoolbag and wore the civil T-shirt on top of my school uniform. And then with a smile on my face, I rang the bell of Rishabh's home. His mother opened the gate and was shocked to see me in school uniform.

'Good morning, Auntie,' I said.

'Good morning, beta. Why you are in the school uniform? I mean to say, except for the T-shirt, you're in your school uniform, and you are even carrying a bag.'

'Actually, Auntie, I was not sure that there was a party or not. Rishabh told me once about the party, and even he didn't say it seriously. I thought he may be joking, and I also did not have Rishabh's number. That's why, Auntie, I am in this dress. And I am even carrying my school shirt and tie because if there will be no party, then I can wear them and can go back to school.'

'Oh, so nice. It means you came here with both options.'

'Yah, correct.'

I entered the home and enjoyed the party. As Rishabh cut the cake, we started throwing cake and putting cream on each other's face. After enjoying for two to three hours, we sat together for lunch. I saw that the food was non-veg as well as veg. I ate veg food. Rishabh asked me the reason for eating the veg food. I told him that I will tell the reason but only after lunch. After finishing lunch, we sat on the couch. Rishabh immediately asked me the reason for eating veg food.

'Yes, my reason is simple. I don't want to give pain to anyone.'

'What do you mean? We are not giving pain to anyone.'

'You are, but you do not realize that. Today, we have enjoyed a lot. You ate nice food, non-veg, but you have also made someone cry. Guys, I was also non-vegetarian, but I stopped it just by reading a single article which was published in *HT Education* and was written by Swati Jain. The topic of the article was "Cruelty—A Slow Poison", wherein she mentioned very nicely about the killing of animals and the cruelty of humans. And by the way, it's your luck that I am carrying that article today. Listen to it carefully.'

Cruelty—A Slow Poison

Human beings are undoubtedly the most intelligent and the powerful of all the creatures on the earth, but does that qualify them to inflict the limitless cruelty, brutality and torture on the dumb innocent animals in the name of experiment, religion, science and business.

Animal cruelty is a worldwide problem rapidly growing in today's so called modern society. Everyday millions of animals are put through horrendous conditions and are put to death for their meat, skin hair sometimes even blood and a hell a lot more. In this so called age of science, the poor little creature are put through living hell; there skins are peeled off their body when they are still alive; they get burnt in the scientific experiment; hair are literally scratched from their body; some companies even go as far as to place metal wires and rods in the living animals head in the name of experiment. With so many invention finding, advancement in technology, if still these little creatures have to face such traumatizing death, it's a shame! Shame on humanity! Shame on science!

In the case of animals, as in the case of men, it is only justifiable to inflict pain in order to obtain some greater good, which compensates for the evil of the pain, I would say the discovery of metals, thousands of chemicals and other material is a waste if it still needs the hair and skin of animals to fulfill the human needs. Just imagine for a moment somebody peeling your skin off your body, feel the pain and pledge to stop this inhuman act.

Animals product does fulfill the human needs but at the peak of inhuman levels of brutality. Is it right to inflict pain and cruelty on helpless animals in the name of science; in the making of new cosmetic and other products; for sports; for making mew records. Is there life so priceless to be scarified at no cost? Can't we live without these acts of brutality? Are they so necessary?

How would our world be without animals? How would be our nature without birds? What would be of our world without these beautiful inhabitants of nature?

Human beings are killing animals for their greed without realizing that these little creature are a part of the natural or the so called scientific life cycle; if these animals become extinct so would the man himself. Cruelty is that slow poison with which man is digging his grave himself. So if not for the happiness of the animals but for the human sake, this cruelty must be put to an end. Be the voice for the creature who cannot speak up for themselves. Save the lives of this beautiful little creature and save the mother earth who is crying at the horrendous death of its little innocent beings. (Swati Jain)

'Yes, guys, I hope you all have understood my feelings and my reason behind eating veg food. Guys, imagine the situation if someone is peeling your skin from your body. Just realize the pain.'

'Yah, I understand your feelings. But nothing is going to change. You have stopped today. I will stop, but is it sufficient to save animals' lives? There are millions of people who are non-vegetarian. They also have to stop. Even if we stop eating, nothing is going to change. So it's better to eat,' Rishabh said.

'Yah, you are right. The same thought came into my mind also. But, guys, it was not for the sake of the animals but for the sake of humanity that I thought I should stop this. I didn't think what others are doing. I imagined myself whenever I would go to the retailers to buy mutton, chicken, or fish—whatever it may be. They will just hold the animal however they want, and at first, they will cut the neck. Have you ever thought who is responsible for this? If I have not demanded the retailer to kill it, it may happen that particular animal may survive for some more days. That animal was killed just because of me. I have done a big sin. And only I was responsible for this sin. So at last, I decided that I will not do any more sin. Let the others do what they are doing. One day they will also change.

'And, guys, one more thing inspired me to take this step. It was a poem written in the book of Sean Covey. I don't remember the poem, but I can say in a few words exactly what the poem meant to say. Like in childhood, we dreamed of changing the world, but we couldn't then. As we grew, we decided to shorten our sights to changing the country, then society, then family. And at last, when we are on the deathbed and are unable to change the family too, then we think, "Perhaps if I had changed myself first, then with the help of example, I might have influenced my family. And who knows? Maybe with their encouragement, I might have changed the world." Guys, from this poem I have learned that at first I would have to change myself and then the world will change.'

'Thanks. You have given us a nice lesson today. You are really a brilliant guy. You always taught us the good as well as the bad things. And this behaviour towards animals shows your empathy. Akash, we also promise you that from today we will also stop eating non-veg. In fact, I will also share these ideas with my friends' relatives and everyone.'

'I have an idea. Why not to put this article in the school notice board or distribute it to every child in the school so that their parents can even know about this?' Rishabh said.

'Yah, you are right, but for this, we will have to talk to the principal of the school.'

'Yah, we will talk, but our principal is Bengali, and their main food is rice and fish. If we will talk to her, she may deny us. It will be better if we will ask the help of our Hindi teacher, who is already vegetarian. He will support us to distribute it, and he may even talk to the principal instead of us,' Sumant said.

'Yah, Akash. Tomorrow we are going to talk to Rajesh Sir,' Rishabh said.

'Okay, guys, it's four forty-five. I have to go, and you all know that I will have to go home in my school van only.'

I immediately came out and went back to the same place where I had changed my attire early in the morning. I again wore the school uniform and went to the school van. The driver of the bus didn't even notice that I came from another route. I fooled him very easily, but when I was dropped back at home, I was a little bit scared because my sister would take out my tiffin box from my bag each day and she would see the civil T-shirt in my bag. Then many questions might arise.

The problem was how to hide the T-shirt, but I immediately got an idea. I took out my T-shirt from my bag and kept it properly behind my shoulders, and then I wore my bag very tightly. The T-shirt was not visible. As I rang the bell, my sister opened the door. I went inside and put the T-shirt on the table. Nobody noticed me. I made a fool of my family members, and I even enjoyed the birthday party.

I changed my attire and quickly sent an SMS to Anshika.

'Hey, sweetheart! Wassup?'

Anshika: 'I'm fine. I was just reading a novel.'

Akash: 'You are so cute and cool, angel.'

Anshika: 'Do you know what you are saying, ha?'

Akash: 'Yah, I know what I am saying, angel. You are mine. I can say you are my angel. I love you.'

Anshika: 'I lve u too, but ha, don't call me by this name in front of anyone, or else it will become a topic of discussion.'

Akash: 'Yah sure, janeman tumhari sifarish salakhon pe.
Akhir apse milke hi to ehsaas hua hai
Ki pyar to ham bhi kar sakte hain.'
Dil to ham bhi de sakte hai
Bas aap kaho ek bar
Aap ke liye to hum apni jaan bhi de sakte hai.'

Anshika: 'Aww shayari kahan se churayi? ☺ ;)'

Akash: 'Janeman aisi hazaron shayariyaan

Tum pe var du

Tum bas sath rah aur farmao

Tumhare liye chand tare bhi tod lu.'

Anshika: 'I never knew that you are soo gud in all this also.'

Akask: 'Sunshine abhi meri khubhiyan tumne dekhi hi kahan hain?'

Anshika: 'Ohhkk, Mr Prince Charming, hum bhi dekhenge n yaa aab sone do varna kal school nahin aa paungi.'

Akash: 'Okay. Goodnight, love you, and do come to school.'

Again my phone beeped, and there was a message and the message read: 'Goodnight, love you too. And yes, sir, I will come to school for sure.'

After reading this message, I was lost in a dream. I was not able to sleep because my brain was receiving only the messages sent by her: 'Mr Prince Charming', 'Mr Prince Charming', and 'Mr Prince Charming'.

Persuading the Teacher

Next morning as I woke up, I saw a message from her which read: 'Good morning. U awake?'

I immediately replied to her. 'Good morning to you too. I woke up, but you made me sleepless the whole night. I was not able to sleep just because of you.'

As I went to brush my teeth, my phone beeped again with a message which read: 'Don't blame me, bhul gaye woh din. You taught me never to blame anyone because we ourselves are only responsible for our each and every fault. Kya hua unn philosophical bato ka. Did you forget it? First apply all those things in your own life before you teach anyone else :p.'

I quickly replied to her. 'Accha thik hai babaaa. Forgive me.'

After sending this message, I quickly took a bath and got ready for school. I took the article and went to school. After reaching school, I first met Rajesh Sir so that the article could be placed on the notice board. As I told him about this, he agreed with me immediately to put the article on the notice board. But when I requested him to distribute this to every student, he became a little bit reluctant to accept it.

'Sir, please talk to Principal Ma'am. Sir, it's not going to affect the students too much by putting this article on the notice board. Students are not going to take it seriously, and moreover, sir, only 40 per cent to 50 per cent of the students are going to read this. And even, sir, from these students,

96

only seniors are going to understand the matter because I know the condition of our junior section. Their English is not so good.

'And, sir, it will be better if this article will get translated into the Bengali and Hindi languages. And then, sir, give the assignment to the students to show this paper to their neighbours to make them understand, and then, sir, one more paper should be given to students in which they will take the signature of their neighbours. Sir, this will not only help us spread the knowledge, even students will get interested in these activities, and sir, the school will also earn fame in the market because, sir, it is a kind of social welfare.'

'Yah, your points are all true. It will be very helpful for the students as well as for the school also to get admissions in the new session. I will talk to the principal today, and ha, don't worry. Think that the job is done. I will give my best, and I know that she will agree with it.'

'Thank you, sir.'

Trnnngggg . . . The bell rang, and our awaited recess began. Most of the students rushed from the ground floor to the fourth floor. Some went to the grounds to play catch. Some went to the canteen to get cold drinks and delicious food, like cakes, pizzas, ice cream. But the chole bhature was one of the most in-demand food in our canteen just because it is delicious and is the cheapest food in the canteen, costing only 5 rupees for five bhatures and unlimited chole.

And moreover, the canteen was one of the most dangerous places for juniors because seniors would rob their food easily in the crowded place and juniors wouldn't even notice them. So even some went to the staircase to hide themselves and eat the food there so that no one could snatch the food from them.

And the most common thing was that some guys would peep inside the girls' washroom by climbing the wall of the boys' toilet, and it was possible just because the washrooms were right next to each other. They were only separated by a wall which was built in half.

And last, the lovers' points, which were seen in each floor's corridor; girls and boys would hold hands and talk together with smiles on their faces, and as the teacher passed by, they would start talking about studies. This was one of the most common habits of lovers. I also came out of class and was feeling lonely just because I was in search of my angel, who was missing from the class.

After the bell, her missing from the class always made me uncomfortable, and even for a single day, if she would not meet me at recess, then it would become impossible for me to swallow even a drop of water. All my activeness would vanish, and my bright face would turn pale if she would not meet me. And most of all, that particular day would go to waste because my foremost objective for coming to school was to meet her, to talk to her, and moreover, to woo her.

I was walking in the corridor and thinking this entire thing so that the particular day would not go to waste. I suddenly saw a crowd in front of the notice board; all of them were fighting one another to read something. I did not know what was there on the notice board, but I was sure that it must be that particular article, 'Cruelty–A Slow Poison'. As I reached near the notice board, I saw there were two papers—one was the article, and the other was something else. As I was about to read it, I got a glimpse of my angel, and after seeing her, I forgot to read the notice. I approached her to talk.

'Hi, Anshika, how is this article?'

'It's awesome.'

Ttrrnngg . . .

'Oh shit!'

'What happened?'

'Nothing. The bell rang.'

'No problem. We will talk through SMS.'

'Yah.'

As she went away, I thought my whole recess went badly; I was not able to read the notice, nor was I able to talk to her. The classes began, but I was absent-minded just because of what happened at recess.

After reaching home, as I was splashing my face with water, my phone beeped, and it was a message from her, which read: 'Are you there at home? Then msg me if you are free because I am also free and want to talk you.'

Akash: 'I am only at home. Tell me.'

Anshika: 'I know you are angry with me because I didn't meet you at recess. I'm sorry for that. Actually, I was just crossing from there. I saw the crowd, and I went there to read the notice. Please pardon me.'

Akash: 'It's okay, baby. Actually, it was my fault also. I only came late. If I had been in time, then it would not have happened. I'm sorry too.'

Anshika: 'It's okay, *jannu*. Leave this entire thing. Hmm. Yah, I remember you are a big hypocrite.'

Akash: 'Me, a hypocrite? Not possible at all.'

Anshika: 'Yah, you. What have you told Sumant to tell me?'

Akash: 'Nothing.'

Anshika: 'Oh . . . you started telling a lie. I also have never thought that you will tell lie.'

Akash: 'Leave all these things. Just tell me what he said.'

Anshika: 'He told me that you told him to tell me that you have talked to the teacher to put this article on the notice board, and you even told him that I should praise you because you are doing a nice work.'

Akash: 'First of all, I didn't say anything to him, and secondly, how can you relate this thing with hypocrisy?'

Anshika: 'I said you are a hypocrite because you only told me that a good person never pranks or jokes on others and never praises himself. And you are breaking your own rules.'

Akash: 'Oh, you remember each and every thing, and by the way, I didn't say this entire thing, I swear. Sumant might have been kidding with you.'

Anshika: 'Okay. If you are saying, mere janeman, then I have to believe it, but ha, I told him never to crack a joke like this. We will meet tomorrow. Goodbye and lve you.'

Akash: 'Goodbye and lve u 2, my sweetheart angel.'

After sending this message, I went to the grounds and met Sumant as usual at that particular place.

'Hi, Sumant. What the hell are you doing, man?'

'Who the hell is doing what?'

'You.'

'Me? Not possible at all.'

'Sumant, please don't be so innocent. What did you say to Anshika?'

'Oh, you are talking about her. Yah, I just told her some fake thing about you.'

'Do you think you have done the right thing?'

'I was just kidding with her. Why are you so serious, man?'

'Sumant, you were kidding, but she had taken it seriously. She was arguing with me regarding the matter you told her.'

'I'm sorry, yaar, but my intention was not to cause an argument between you both.'

'It's okay, but ha, tell her tomorrow that you were kidding with her. And, Sumant, please don't crack a joke like this next time with her. Bye.'

After taking dinner, I went to sleep, but before going to sleep, I messaged her because I knew that I couldn't sleep without talking her.

'Hi, Anshika. What's up?'

I immediately got a message. It seemed that she would always keep her mobile with her so that she can reply to a message very fast.

The message showed: 'I'm reading. It's a very interesting and romantic novel.'

Akash: 'Oh . . . it means you are reading a love story. Can you read a line from it for me?

Anshika: 'Obviously, the most interesting and important line for me is "If you like a girl and if you know why you like that girl, then it's a crush, and if you like a girl and if you don't know why you like that girl, then it's love".'

After reading this message, I remembered the old days when I was in doubt of whether I loved her or not, but the message made me realize again that it was true love between us because I also don't know why I like her.

Akash: 'Thanks, baby. Your message is a very interesting line, and ha, you didn't tell me what the notice on the board was except for that article.'

Anshika: 'It was not for us. It was for the twelfth class, and the notice was related to OBCs.'

Akash: 'OBCs? Please tell me clearly what it was about.'

Anshika: 'It was said in the notice that seniors should take the board exam very seriously, especially those who are not OBCs because after school, there are reservations for the OBC students. And if the other castes will not be able to perform well, then they can't get admission in a good college because there are limited seats and huge competition.'

Akash: 'Thanks, baby. You are really a cool girl. You always give me all information, and ha, I'm sorry because this will be my last message. I am feeling very sleepy. Goodnight and lve u a lot.'

After sending this message, I remembered that only two days were left before our anniversary. On 7 March, it was going to be a year for us. I was in doubt of what to give her as a surprise. But then a good idea struck my mind, and it was to meet her on the 7th in front of her house.

First Anniversary

I woke up early on the morning of 7 March and got ready to leave home without informing my parents. I wrote on a paper that I was going for cycling and warming up the body and kept the paper on the table, and I went off. Firstly, I bought a red rose and went to her home. After reaching there at 7 a.m. sharp, I messaged her.

'Good morning. U awake?'

After a second, I got a message.

'Good morning to you too. I woke up, and I have even taken a bath. I am not lazy like you.'

Akash: 'You mean to say I am lazy?'

Anshika: 'Yah, you are lazy, selfish, and you are even a very forgetful person.'

Akash: 'What are you saying? Me, *bhullakar*? It's next to impossible. Do you remember what today is?'

Anshika: 'Yah, I remember today is our first anniversary. A year has passed.'

Akash: 'Yah, I too know that. That's why I asked you if you remember or not.'

Anshika: 'I can't believe you at all. It must be another matter you are talking about. If you had known, then instead of saying good morning, you would have greeted me last night at twelve o'clock. I was waiting for your message till one o'clock.'

Akash: 'Oh . . . I remembered. Don't you believe it now? Do you think I am telling a lie?'

Anshika: 'Yah, you are telling a lie. I can't believe you at all because you are a very forgetful person.'

Akash: 'Okay. If you don't believe me, just open the window of the first room on your ground floor.'

After sending this message, I went in front of the window and stood there for a minute. Suddenly, she opened the window. I was stunned after seeing her. She looked so gorgeous than I have ever seen her before. She was in a bathrobe. Her hair was wet, and some of her hair fell over her face. She was totally simple and yet gorgeous. It seemed that she had only taken her bath a few minutes before. And she hadn't even changed her attire; she just came to open the window.

'Akash . . . you are here. How is it possible? And how did you come to know my address?'

'Yah, I'm here, and it's for you.'

'Wow . . . A rose. Thank you. You are really very kind. I am sorry for saying all those things. I didn't even realize in my dreams that you will give me such a nice gift. You don't know that your presence on this precious day and that even in the early morning is the biggest and the most beautiful gift in my life. Arré ha, how did you come to know about my address?'

'I will tell you, but is this the right time to ask this entire thing? Will you not invite me inside your home?'

'Arré ha. I forgot. I am sorry for that. But ha tell me what you want from me today.'

'I will tell you, but first, please open the door.'

'Arré ha. But, Akash, Mom and Dad are here at home. It's impossible for you to get in.'

'Please don't say something like that, my dream for today will get shattered into pieces, and ha, *impossible* itself means *I-am-possible*. You just tell me where your parents are.'

'They are on the first floor.'

'Then there is no problem at all. You just tell me where your room is.'

'I am in my room.'

'Then its fine. You just open the door. I will come into your room, then we will close the door of the room, and no one is going to know that.'

'But, Akash, it's risky.'

'So what? Don't you remember "dar ke aage jeet hai"?'

'Oh, please stop your dialogue. If my father finds this out, then he will kick me outside this home.'

'Then it's fine. We will run away. And we will enjoy our whole life staying in the same room and spending our school, college, and married life together. Will you please open it?'

After insisting with her for a long time, she agreed, and finally she opened the door without even making a single noise of anything. I entered the home and saw a tulsi tree at the corner of the wall in the corridor and a big pond with green water in it.

'Come from here. Keep your shoes there, and please don't make a single noise.'

'Yah, I know that we are doing something wrong.'

'Wait here.'

'But why?'

'Let me arrange my room.'

'Leave it, yaar. If I stand here, someone may catch me. Let's go inside. Lock the door, and then do whatever you want to do.'

'Yah, you are right. Come in, but ha don't look at my bed. It is on the right side. It's a humble request from me.'

As we entered the room, she quickly closed the door and went towards her bed. I moved towards the left side of the room, but unfortunately, I got a glimpse of her from the mirror placed on the left side of the room hiding her lingerie below the mattress. A smile came on my face, but I didn't say anything to her.

'Yah, my innocent and culprit boyfriend, now you can see.'

I looked towards her bed; it looked very nice, and it made me realize that she was very well and good in managing the household things. And I even dreamed that my mom would be very blissful if I married her because her wish was the same; she wanted me to have a wife who is good in household work.

'Yah, now say to me what you want.'

'A hug and a kiss, nothing else.'

'What? Are you mad?'

'Yah.'

I moved towards her and pulled her towards me. Then I moved my hands towards her waist; it was very slim and tender, and at last, I hugged her. Her body was smoother, softer, and warmer than velvet. The smell of the perfume on her body forced me to hold her body as long as I could.

I looked into her eyes. 'Baby, I promise you on this special day that I will be always faithful to you. And'—I went on my knees and proposed her—'will you be my soulmate? Will you marry me? Do you want to share those precious moments of your life with me?'

She was almost in tears, tears of happiness, and not able to utter a word.

'Yes,' she said, blushing all over. Her cheeks had turned rose red. She sat down and hugged me tight.

And then it happened.

Her fragrance overpowered my senses. Her warmth and her love just added to the flavour.

Those pink lips were just inches away. Her deep, long breaths told me that she wanted me to kiss her, and then we kissed. Her lips tasted so sweet. I had always fantasized about kissing her.

My hand moved towards her boobs. She resisted and caught my hand, still kissing me passionately. But her voice clearly showed her willingness. I opened her bathrobe. She was wearing a bra.

Her breathing grew rapid.

I unclasped the hook of her bra. Ohh god, she had the perfect breasts. Everything about her was so perfect—the way she kissed, the way she moaned when I squeezed her breasts.

'Anshika, beta!'

'Oh shit, Mom is here. I told you it may be risky, but you didn't listen to me.'

'Arré, leave all these things. Tell me the place where to hide,' I said, trying to act cool while she was trying to put back her clothes.

'Hmm . . . Ya go under the bed.'

I praised her idea and hid myself under the bed.

'Beta, didn't you wake up?' her mom said.

'Yah, Mom, wait a minute.'

She opened the door. I saw her mom's leg which had a *payal* and a black thread tied on the left leg.

'Why did you open the door so late?'

'Actually, Mom, I was just setting the bed.'

'Fine. But how did this red rose come here? It was not here yesterday.'

I was shocked as her mother talked about the rose.

'Mom, I bought it yesterday, only it was in my bag, but I took it out just now.'

'Oh. But, beta, I think you are hiding something. At first, you opened the door late, and now the rose is placed here. And you are telling me that you bought it yesterday, but it seems very fresh. If it was from yesterday, then now it would have got withered.'

'Arré, Mom. Don't you believe your daughter?'

'It's okay.'

Her mom went off.

'Akash, come out. Go through the back door of the room and be there in the corridor until I say go.'

I followed her instructions and stood there waiting for her instructions. Then suddenly, I heard the sound of her mom's voice.

'Anshika, whose shoes are here in the corridor?'

Anshika shouted, 'Go.'

I rushed from there, took my shoes, and flew away from there. While riding the cycle, hundreds of thoughts came into my mind. I only thought of her. What excuse would she give to her mom? I thought of messaging her, but I just can't because of fear. In the late evening, I lost my patience and messaged her.

'Hi. What's up? Is it all okay?'

After a minute, my phone beeped, and the message read: 'Yah, it's fine now. The matter is solved. But, plz don't ask for details. Tomorrow at recess, I am going to share them with you.'

After reading this message, I was totally relaxed and was desperately waiting for recess the next day.

At recess the next day, as usual I was waiting for my baby only at that place where we usually meet. Suddenly, she came and spoke to me.

'Akash, we took a very large and wrong step. If my mother had known that you were there in my room, then you don't know what would have been my situation and even yours.'

'I know it would have been the worst condition for you, but what the hell can your parents do to me?'

'You don't know my father. He may put an FIR against you for illegally entering my home and molesting me.'

'Oh, madam, I didn't do anything wrong with you. It was with your consent only. Don't blame me like this.'

'Be cool, Akash. I am not blaming you for this entire thing. My father can do things like these and may even complain.'

'Okay. Leave this entire thing. You just say to me how you handled the matter as I went away.'

'As you went through the back door, my mother came into the room to ask about the shoes. She took me with her to show me the shoes, but by the time we reached there, you had vanished from our home along with your shoes. And my mother was shocked as the shoes were not there. I acted as if

I didn't know anything about you, and I asked Mom about the shoes. She was dumbstruck.'

'Angel, I hope you will never forget our first celebration of our anniversary. And ha why did you and your mother have black thread on your left leg? May I know the reason behind it?'

'Yah, I will never forget today. It was a very adventurous day. But may I know why you are asking such strange things? The reason is not anything special. It's simple. No one can put an evil eye.'

'You believe in this thing? My Anshika believes all these useless things? Believe me, tear it out, and throw it away. Nothing will happen to you.'

'Why should I tear it out? If you can believe in God, then why can't I believe in such things?'

'Oh, if you don't know, then please don't say it. I don't believe in God. I don't believe in anything.'

'You mean to say you are an atheist? Can you prove it? How can I believe in you, and how can you prove that this entire thing is useless?'

'See, I cannot prove it to you unless and until you apply it in your own practical life. I do believe it because I have applied it in my own practical life, like at morning assembly. I used to say "god aaj ka din accha jaye", but later on, I started saying "aaj ka din kharab jaye god"—and not only for a single day, but for many days I have said this. And on those particular days, nothing went wrong with me, and from then on, I started believing that from the way we behave, the way we do hard work, the way we commit mistakes, in the same manner, we get results.

'God is not responsible for this entire thing. I have seen many fools who pray to God only when they require help, or if they are in a problem, then they pray to God like anything. And I hope you have seen this in our school also. Many of the students would pray to God just on the day of examination, and when there is no exam, they don't even see the face of God. They would pass by from there.

'And, Anshika, not only this. I believe you have heard superstitions that no one should cross the road if a cat has crossed it, no one should look at their face in a broken mirror, no one should put their slippers in an inverse position, and even many more. I have tried all these things in my practical life. That's why I am saying don't believe them at all. All these are useless things. And even now also, if you want more proof, then obey all this in your own practical life.'

'Okay, I will think it over. By the way, you preach a lot. Don't you think so?'

'I don't think so, and if I am preaching a lot, then there is no harm at all. I am only preaching to my mate who is going to be a spouse of mine in the future. I want that my spouse should have the same opinion like me, and ha, we should not feel shy to share knowledge. If we have some good knowledge, then we should share it with everyone so that they can also know about all those matters.'

'Okay, babaa. Thik hai. Thank you and bye.'

'Arré, where are you going? I didn't ask you to go. At least, say something.'

'What do I say? I don't have anything more to share. And by the way, you can also say something.'

'Actually, I speak less and do more.'

'Ohh . . . that means you are talking about yesterday's incident. You have done nothing great. In privacy, everyone can do it, and moreover, you did it just because I allowed you to.'

'Hahaha . . .' She laughed.

'Hmm, really?'

'Yah,' she said.

I saw the time; only ten seconds were left, and even no one was minding where we were standing. I moved closer towards her, kissed her, and walked away. From a distance, when I looked back at her, she was staring at me with wide eyes while keeping her hand on her cheek where I kissed her.

OBC Leads to . . .

The next day, I met all my friends at recess at the canteen because we were having a plan to booze up on Valentine's Day, which was on the next day on Sunday. So we were enjoying the day. After taking soft drinks, we sat together and had a discussion on everything.

'Hi, guys. We discussed everything and enjoyed a lot, but can anyone say the answer to my question "For whom is Valentine's Day celebrated?" I mean, Valentine's Day is celebrated especially for what purpose?'

'Hi. Do you think we are fools? Or do you want to prove that you are a fool, that's why you are asking this question?' Rishabh said.

'Arré, please understand me. You just tell me the answer, then I will disclose my views.'

'It's simple, yaar. The day is celebrated for lovers. Many of the guys even propose on this day only,' Sumant said.

'Fine. Any more answers? Guys, your answers are right, but even we should wish a happy Valentine's Day to those who have brought changes into our lives. The word *valentine* actually means "the one whom you love or whom you are attracted to". I mean to say that "whom you are attracted to" can also be seen in a positive manner. Likewise today, we are here, we can see this beautiful world, and we are literate. *Literate* in a sense means not only those who are able to read and write. *Literate* means those who are able to read, write, and even understand.

'We have our own perception, personality, ethical values, and even many more things just because of our parents, teachers, and elders. We have learned all these things from them only. Why not greet them first? The foremost responsibility of ours is to greet our parents, who have taught us to walk, speak, and do many more things, then the teachers who gave us knowledge.

'Friends, in today's modern days, we enjoy our lives to the fullest because of our parents. They help us financially with our expenses, but we tell them lies, making fools out of them, and spending our money on girls so that we can propose to them and can make them our girlfriends. And later, we romance with them, and we even wish a happy Valentine's Day to them only. Guys, I hope we all know that most of the romantic relationships between boys and girls are fleeting because 80 per cent of lovers break up within a month or a year.

'They break up just because they don't know the actual meaning of love. If there is a minor argument, they decide to break up. Guys, this is not love. Love is something which we have to learn from our parents. I know we all have done naughtiness, wrongdoing, or many other things which have hurt our parents. And for these mistakes, they even beat us and punish us, but they never leave us, do they? Never.

'And ha, many times, even when they beat us first, they would then ask, "Jada to nahi laga?" And then they would do treatment for that. This is true love.

'Hmm, correct,' evryone said in unison.

There was a pause for a few minutes, and everyone started staring at me only as if I have said something strange. Sumant was the first to break the silence.

'Hey, Akash, have you read the notice related to OBCs?'

'Yah, I have read it, but I am totally against it.'

'But why? Just because you don't belong to OBC?'

'No, yaar, it's nothing like that. See, guys, it was mentioned that twelfth-class students should prepare well for getting admission into a good college because of more competition. And moreover, some seats were reserved for OBCs, so they should work harder. I am totally satisfied with the view that there is more competition so students should work hard because lack of competition leads to shirkers. And if there will be a competition, then students will only work hard.

'But I am not satisfied with the view that the seats are reserved for OBCs. I don't know why the government has put such a kind of reservation. It is fine for them who are suffering from penury. On one side, we are thinking of unity among Indians, and on another side, we are just dividing Indians on the basis of caste. The people should be divided on the basis of effort and dedication towards their goals, not on the basis of caste. Yes, the preference can be given to handicapped people, so these things disunite the people. And I can't even understand that. The OBC students are also human like us, then why only to them?

'Moreover, the reservation demoralizes the good students, like when an efficient student who secured 96 per cent is not able to get admission in Shri Ram College just because some seats are reserved for OBCs only. And the students who had secured only 91 per cent are getting admission just because they are OBCs. This is total injustice, and this injustice will lead to the breaking of dreams of efficient students, and it will not only break their dreams, but it even demoralizes them and kills their efficiency and their willingness to work. And, guys, this is not the end. The inflation is also responsible for this.'

'Oh, how can you relate this to inflation in India? It is just because of the fact that there is more demand and lesser supply,' Ananya said.

'Yah, that's true, but reservation is also responsible. Imagine for a moment, if a guy secures 96 per cent, it proves that he is more efficient then the guy who secured 91 per cent. And if that efficient guy is not able to get admission in a good college, therefore he will not get a chance for campus selection. Moreover, I hope you all know that big companies with good packages come to good colleges only because they know that these colleges have efficient students. And the companies recruit them as managers and give them a good package with the hope that the manager is efficient.

'Now imagine if the guy with the 96 per cent would get the job. He is more efficient and has more skill, so he can get the job done through others more nicely. He has more knowledge on which resources and technology should be utilized and how the resources should be utilized in the optimum manner. And if the manager has such skills, then the cost of the production of goods in which the firm is dealing will be lesser, and if the cost of production is lesser, then the selling price will also be lesser. And if the selling price is lesser, then there will be no inflation.

'Guys, I hope you understand my views. And this is not the end. You can even relate this to penury.'

'Hmm, great,' Anshika said.

'Guys, let's move. We all are late. Recess had already ended five minutes ago,' I said.

Valentine's Day

After coming back from school, I was very happy because tomorrow was Valentine's Day and the school was closed as it was a Sunday. I was very much agog for the clock to strike twelve o'clock because Anshika and I had a competition with each other on who would greet the other first. After seven hours, finally the watch showed 11.57 p.m. I started writing the message.

'Happy Valentine's Day, angel, I love you. You are the reason for the smile on my face and heartbeats in my heart. I promise to love you till the end.'

At the time when I had just finished typing it and was going to send it, my phone beeped, and it was a message from an unknown number which read: 'I love you very much from the core of my heart. Don't ignore it. Please reply.'

I thought angel was kidding with me by sending a message in such a way that it seemed she was saying 'I love you' for the first time. I immediately sent my text to this new number. But soon, I got another message from Anshika's number.

'I love you, and I won the bet. I said to you earlier also that you will lose this bet, but you didn't listen to me.'

I was stunned after reading this, and I became doubtful. Whose message did I receive in the beginning? If this was Anshika's message, then who sent me the first message? And I even replied 'I love u' without knowing the number and just by thinking that Anshika had messaged me.

As I was thinking all this, I received another message from the new number which read: 'I proposed to you, and you accepted me. Then why fear and wait? Wouldn't you like to talk to me on such an auspicious day?'

After reading this message, I lost my patience. I immediately pressed the menu button to call her, but again I received another message. It was from Anshika, and it read: 'You lost the bet. It doesn't mean you will not talk. Call me first. I am very much agog to talk you.'

After reading this, I immediately called Anshika.

'Hi, Anshika, lve u. And ha, please don't put chilli on my wounds.'

'Hahahaha. You are so timid. You get fearful of me so easily.'

'No no. It's nothing like that. Leave this entire thing. Say: "aajkakya plan hai."'

'I do not have any plans at all, and ha, don't even try to come to my home today in the morning. I don't want to take any risk at all.'

'Angel, why not go for a date?'

'What?'

'Yah, why are you so shocked? I will not come to your home. You have to go somewhere, and I will be there.'

'Where?'

'You tell me—wherever it is suitable for you.

'No, not at all. Do you want to get me killed?'

'Arré, please na!'

'Okay! Any nearest one, and I will be there for an hour only.'

'Okay, it's fine. Tomorrow at 9 p.m. sharp in the Penguin restaurant. But, Anshika, why for an hour only?'

'I'm coming. Say thanks for that, and by the way, I'm coming without any permission. My parents will be out and I have to be back, home before my parents arrive.'

'Fine. Goodnight, and ha, love you.'

'Love you too.'

As I ended my call, I dialled the unknown number.

'Hello, Akash,' a girl said from the other side.

I understood that the voice was Akansha's. I was surprised to know that she had proposed to me.

'Yah.'

'Why did you take so much time to call me? I was waiting for you for so long. Akash, I love you very much, and ha, don't take it as a joke. It's true.'

I thought of denying her proposal and telling her sorry, but then I thought it was also my mistake that I accepted her. I couldn't deny her directly. I had to make her realize that I was in love with someone else, and if I denied her now, she might get angry. She might say a lot of bad things to me, and our friendship might also break. That was why I replied to her very nicely.

'I didn't say that you were joking. I'm sorry for calling you late. Actually, I was too busy in something personal.'

'Something personal? What do you mean by that?'

'Why should I say that? Will you be ready to show your private thing?'

'Oh sorry.'

'Yah, good. I'm also sorry because I behaved wrongly. Actually, I am in a sleepy mood. I will talk you tomorrow morning.'

'Why can't you talk this morning?'

'Okay. Sorry, madam. I forgot that it's twelve thirty now. I will only talk later, so let me sleep. Goodnight.'

'Goodnight and love you.'

The next day as I woke up, I first went to Sumant's home to tell him all the incidents and what happened late that night. I saw him reading a newspaper, and the front page showed that only 1 per cent of India's population is below the poverty line. They are not even able to take a meal twice in a day, and they sleep in hunger.

'By the way, I didn't come to preach to you. If you feel bad, I'm sorry for that. I came here just to share my problem. Sumant, please help me. I am in big trouble.'

'What happened, dude? You're a person who teaches us, and today you are in a problem?'

'Yah.'

And I told him all the incidents and what happened to me last night.

'See, if you have done a mistake, you have to regret it. I can only suggest to you to say the truth to Akansha as fast possible. Otherwise, it may happen that if Anshika or Akansha will come to know about this, then they will think that you are a trickster, and it may happen that you may lose your friendship with both of them, and love will be too far.'

'You are right. I know that it may happen. That's why I came to you, and you are helping me. It's disgusting. Give me some idea so that I can console her.'

'Yah, I got it. Why not go for a picnic after the exam? You can even console her there.'

'But where?'

'In Water Parks.'

'But how? If I will be going, then I have to spend time with Anshika only, and how can I talk to Akansha in Anshika's presence? And how can I even stay with Anshika in front of Akansha? If I will spend time with Anshika, then she may get angry.'

'Is it compulsory to stay with your queen? Can't we lads spend time together? I mean, we are all friends. We'll be together. We will all be in a group. No one will spend time alone with a girl. Let's first go for a picnic, then we will handle the situation. Okay?'

'Done.'

After coming back home, I informed all my friends about the picnic plan, and I even requested them to study hard so that our picnic programme would not get cancelled. I dusted my books and started studying so that I could also secure good marks. But as I started reading the books, I was not able to concentrate because I was thinking of Valentine's Day, which I was going to celebrate with Anshika that night. I was very much agog to see her that night and spend time with her. After waiting for ten long painful hours, I quickly dressed up and went to the restaurant and started waiting for her.

After ten minutes, I saw her coming towards me. She looked very stunning, hot, and innocent too. Her attire was perfectly suitable for her body. She was in blue jeans and a pink shirt. As I saw her, I lost my patience, and I only thought of hugging her there and then, but I controlled myself. She came in front of me with a smile on her face. She held my palm, and we started approaching towards the doors of the restaurant. While walking, I felt that we were a young married couple who were holding hands tightly and going for their first dinner after nuptials.

As we walked ten steps ahead, Anshika cried, 'Shit! Leave me.'

As I let go of her palm, she rushed away from there and hid herself behind the wall. I also ran towards her.

'What happened, baby?'

'Mom and Dad are here.'

'Where?'

'Inside the restaurant.'

'What?'

'Yes.'

'Are those your parents?'

'Yah.'

'But, baby, your parents seem very romantic, but you are always afraid to spend time with me. I think they came here to enjoy their Valentine's Day with a good dinner. That's why they didn't take you, and they even didn't inform you,' I said.

'See, listen, I am not going for dinner any more, I am extremely sorry.'

'But why, baby? We can go to another place.'

'Is it nearby?'

'Hmm.'

'Okay, fine.'

As she agreed to go to another restaurant, I let out a sigh of relief. Particularly in that moment in time, I was totally dumbstruck just because of her annoyance, but now we were here at Regent Restaurant, sitting together for a candlelit dinner. For me, her presence was the best gift from her for Valentine's Day. We both were staring at each other with smiles on our faces; none of us spoke for some minutes. I was just thinking about her face, how God had worked over it so skilfully. This cute small nose and mouth, her eyes that said more than her mouth, her smile, her hair, her earrings, her rings, and her necklace—OMG, literally all were flawless.

Suddenly she spoke up, 'Will you say something? Or will you keep on staring at me?'

'Kya kahu samaj mai kuch aata nahi
Sapno mai tum raheti ho
Abhi bhi tum baithe ho
Bolne ko dil to bahut kuch kaheta hai
Par tumhari sundarta ko dekhkar
Tarrif ke lafz bhi kam par jata hain.' I said.

'Wow! Nice, now listen to me.
Mujhe samaj nahi aata, tum kaise mil gaya
Mujhe samaj nahi aata, tum kaise mil gaya
Mille to mille
Mere dil mai bas gaye.

Don't think yourself as too smart. If you can create a shayri, then I also can,' she said.

'Hmm. Leave it, baby, just tell me what you want to eat.'

'As you wish. Date pe to tum laye ho.'

'Waiter,' I cried. As he came, I ordered a plate of *paneer makkhani* and some *tandoori rotis*.

'Hey, will you be able to afford it? Don't order too much,' she said and even kept her voice low so that the waiter couldn't hear.

'Hmm, I have saved money which I used to get from the club.'

As the waiter went away, she spoke again in a high pitch, 'Don't you think you're spending too much?'

'Leave it, yaar. Just tell me, baby, how good it will be if we marry each other as soon as possible. I really hate studies. I don't know why such kinds of problems are faced only by human beings. First, study, then land a good job, and then marry. Really, I hate such kinds of hurdles.'

'Don't blame me for this entire thing please. Today, we are together because we met in school.'

'Hmm, but leave it, yaar. I don't know why I am asking such a nonsense thing. Today, it's our first date, baby. This is the only right time we should get to know each other. Baby, I have some questions for you, which I had eagerly wanted answered for the last many days just because I want that you would remain happy with me even after marriage. How do you want your husband to be? How many babies do you want? Where do you want to spend your honeymoon?' And I bombarded her with a lot of questions one after another, without even giving her a chance to speak.

Then suddenly she burst out, 'Stop it! What's wrong with you? Why are you only talking about marriage and marriage? It's too far, we are still kids. You will have to wait for at least seven to eight years. And unless and until I become a doctor, I will never marry you—even if you have a good yearly package.'

'Okay. Leave it, baby, please be cool.'

As I said this, our dinner came. We started having it, and we discussed many more things and even made fun of each other by teasing and remembering our old days.

Picnic Preparation

'Oh finally, you came. Where were you? I had been waiting for you for the last ten minutes. Let's go,' Sumant said.

'No. Wait. Please.'

'Why? And for whom are you waiting? Already you are late, and now I have to wait more. I want to play cricket, yaar. After so many days, we have got relief from studies, and the driver may be waiting for us.'

'Arré, leave all these things, yaar. Don't you want to enjoy the picnic?'

'Yah. Why not?'

'Then let me remind her of the picnic.'

'But who? Everybody knows about it.'

'Yah, I know that everybody knows, but Anshika told me to remind her. And you know that if she will not be there in the picnic, then going to the picnic will be useless. You know I love her very much. For me, she is one of the most precious things.'

'Okay. That means I have to leave you alone. I know you want to talk to her alone.'

Peepepeeepeeep . . .

'Oh shit! Akash, we are too late. See? The driver is blowing the horn. We have to move. Otherwise—you know his anger—he may only leave us here, and then it will be more of a problem for us to go home. And thereafter, when we reach home, we have to also get rebuked by our parents.

Akash, let's go. It will be better if you message her after reaching home.'

I realize that his words were true, and I came back home in the school van along with him. After coming home, I immediately changed my clothes and quickly messaged her.

'Angel, where were you after school? I searched for you at each and every place after the exam, and I was even waiting for you outside the main gate to remind you of something, but you didn't come.'

Anshika: 'Oh please, don't tell a lie. You didn't search for me at all places, and even you cannot search for me in all places. And by the way, what did you want to remind me of?'

Akash: 'Oh, madam, I am not telling a lie. It's true. If you don't want to believe me, then don't. Otherwise, I can't force you to believe it, and ha, I was reminding you of the picnic. Be ready for tomorrow. We are all going to Water Parks. We will be waiting for you in Puronopally main road.'

Anshika: 'Ha ha ha ha. Oh, mister, I can prove to you that you didn't search for me at all places. Did you search for me in the girls' washroom? Did you? No, and even you don't have the guts to search for me in the girls' washroom, and even if you have dared it—because I know that you are a very daring guy—then you are mad in my love. And if any other girls caught you, then you will be kicked out from there. You may get two to three slaps, and it may happen that if they go to the authorities, you may get a TC or may be suspended for a month or two. By the way, thank you for reminding me, and ha, don't take it seriously. I was just kidding, and ha, lve you.'

Akash: 'Don't you think you speak too much? Be in the limit. Otherwise, I may leave you. There are lots of girls who are begging for me to accept their proposal, but I denied them just because of u. So it will be better for you to be in the limit.'

I didn't get a response for ten minutes. I thought she was livid. I quickly replied to her.

'Angel, be cool. I was just kidding with you. Why are you not replying to my message? It was just a joke. I lve you vry much, yaar.'

Soon I got another message which read: 'I knew that you lve only me, but I didn't reply to you knowingly just to check your patience level.'

Akash: 'You too smart, na? By the way, goodbye. Lve you and meet you soon.'

Anshika: 'Have a good sleep and lve you too.'

After reading this, I gave a sigh of relief, and I took a nice doze because she was cool and ready to come tomorrow.

Picnic

I was blissful because it was my first picnic with friends. And the second thing was that I was going to say the truth to Akansha, that I love Anshika. It was risky but a relief for me as well if she agrees that on that night I mistakenly messaged her, thinking her as Anshika. I immediately took a bath, ate breakfast, and went to Sumant's home, and from there, we travelled together to meet our remaining friends. But for me, Anshika was the only chief guest to see.

As we reached Puronopally, I saw Anshika, who was already waiting there for us. This time she was in a different attire but looked more gorgeous than any other days. She was in a blue *capri* and yellow tee. A smile came over my face just because a plan struck my mind, which was to take a snap with her while riding the roller coaster.

As we reached there, I didn't spend time alone with Anshika just as Sumant suggested to me earlier because it may lead to problems. I only spent time with the group so that neither Anshika nor Akansha may have doubts. And as for my plan, I had to appeal to Sumant, and he agreed to take a photo. He took the photo in which we looked very cute. After spending three hours, I met Sumant.

'What do I do? You said that you will be handling the situation.'

'Yah, I know I said that. I am just thinking that it will be better to console her after lunch. See? Now Akansha is enjoying a lot with Anshika and Ananya, and if you will say it now, then obviously her mood will be vitiated. And if her mood will be vitiated, then their friends will be able to know that something erroneous has happened with her, and they may force Akansha to say the truth. And if she said it, then our plan will get ruined. So it's better to console her at the last time, not even at lunchtime, but at the time of leaving here.'

'Yah, you are right. Thanks for giving me the precise solution. Let's go for another ride.'

'Yah, you go. I will be there within a minute. See, I have some personal talk with Rishabh also.'

'What? Can't you share it with me?'

'No, yaar. Please understand. Whatever we talked about, if I will say this entire thing to him, how you will feel? You shared your views, thinking of me as your best friend. He also thinks that I am his best friend. That's why I am not sharing with you. And I don't want to destroy anyone's belief on me. I am sorry, but I will share with you one day, I promise.'

As I moved away from there, I saw a serious talk between Rishabh and Sumant, which was making me curious to know the matter. But I couldn't. As I moved a little more ahead, I saw there was a serious talk between Anshika and Ananya. It seems that a very serious matter was going on. And even Anshika made me realize that she was facing some problem. After ten minutes, I saw again there was a serious talk, but this time, it was between Akansha and Ananya. And this time, I saw Akansha crying for the first time. I didn't know what was happening between everyone. I wanted to know each one's matter, but I could not.

After half an hour, I saw Anshika, Ananya, and Akansha were enjoying together, and Sumant and Rishabh were approaching towards me. We again started enjoying together by taking a ride in each and every swing. After an hour, I saw Rishabh and Akansha walking together while holding hands with each other. I was shocked to see them because it was the first time I saw them talking to each other very nicely and even enjoying the picnic. At school, they never behaved in such a manner.

'Hi, Rishabh,' I shouted. 'What happened? Where are you going?'

'I don't even know. She is taking me with her. Actually, I lost the bet. That's why I have to go with her.'

As they went away, I again met Sumant.

'What do I do? Tell me. Finally now the time has come to go back home, and she is not even here to tell me first.'

'What? Akansha is not here? Then where is she?'

'Accident! Accident!'

We heard it from a lad who was shouting in a loud voice. I panicked after hearing about an accident. Sumant and I immediately rushed outside Water Parks. As we approached the main road, we saw a huge throng was there and blood was on the road. It made me fearful. I entered the throng and was traumatized to see that they were Rishabh and Akansha.

Rishabh's body was totally damaged. The blood was oozing out from his stomach. I cried and asked how this happened.

'The truck wheel crossed over his body,' a lad standing behind me said.

I put my hand over Rishabh's nose and realized that he was no more because he had already stopped breathing.

'Come here, Akash,' Sumant shouted.

I ran to where he was.

'Akash, just be here. She needs you.'

As Sumant went towards Rishabh, Akansha cried, 'Akash, I love you. Help me. I want to spend my whole life with you only. Help me.'

I shouted, 'Sumant, where's the ambulance? Call it first.'

'Yah, I have called. It may be arriving.'

I stood up to search for an ambulance. Soon I heard the siren of an ambulance, and I got relieved just because it appeared timely and was not too late. Two people came out from the ambulance with a stretcher on their hands, and they took Akansha and Rishabh to the PVS Nursing Home.

'What do we do? Should we call Anshika and Ananya or go to the hospital?' Sumant said.

'Leave them. Let's first go to the hospital. We will call them from there.'

The cab came. We hired it and travelled to the hospital just behind the ambulance. As we reached the hospital, the doctor declared that Rishabh was dead, and Akansha was shifted to the ICU. The news of Rishabh's death made us dumbstruck. We were totally traumatized. Soon the nurse came from the ICU and told me to fill up the form and to call Akansha's parents and to submit the money as fast as possible. After hearing this, I shuffled towards the reception.

While waddling, I saw Sumant sitting on the corner of the room with tears in his eyes and looking towards the image of God. As I approached the reception, I got the form to fill up. But I was able to complete only 20 per cent of the form because I did not know Akansha very well. I approached Sumant with the form to ask aid from him. Luckily, he had her purse, which he had taken from the main road. And from her purse, I got the ID card of the school, which helped me to fill the address for her and her parents' names.

But the last question on the form put me in doubt of what to write. The question was my relation to the patient. I thought to write 'friend', but then Akansha's tears and pain made me realize how deeply she loved me. I remembered her face and words on the main road when she was delirious with soreness, uttering that she loves me and even that she wanted to spend her whole life with me, and her yelling at me to help her. And the second thought which I had was that while suffering from pain, everybody remembers their parents, but she remembered me, which made me feel that she loves me a lot. And I feel very ignominious because I was deceiving her.

After thinking a lot, I put 'friend' on the blank space for that last question and submitted the form to the receptionist. And the receptionist immediately demanded for the money—one lakh—to be paid within an hour. I was shocked after hearing one lakh because it was a lot for me. I came back to Sumant and took the mobile from her purse, in which she had saved the number of her dad. I called the number.

Ttttrrrrnnnnggggg . . .

'Hello!' The voice came from the other side.

I replied, 'Hello! Uncle, I am Akash, a friend of Akansha's. Please come to PVS Nursing Home.'

'Why?'

'Actually, Uncle, she had an accident. Please come first. We are only waiting for you.'

After saying this, I turned off the phone, and I saw the parents of Rishabh, who came with tears in their eyes. As I approached them, they asked me about Rishabh, and they did not even know that I was the one who called them.

'Beta, can you say in which room Rishabh is, or do you know Akash or Sumant?' Rishabh's father asked me with tears rolling down his cheeks.

'Uncle, I am Akash, and Rishabh is in that room,' I said, pointing towards the room. They immediately rushed towards the room, and Rishabh was lying lifeless on the bed; his corpse was covered with a bed sheet.

I was totally scared about what would happen. If any one of them would remove the bed sheet, then they would be shocked to see the damaged body of Rishabh. I also rushed in, and as his mom touched the head of Rishabh to remove the bed sheet, I cried, 'Stop!'

Everybody started looking towards me. And I requested them not to remove the full bed sheet; instead, they can remove the bed sheet from his face only. They accepted my suggestion, and his mother removed the bed sheet. She started crying loudly. She even started shaking the body of Rishabh and requesting him to say anything.

Suddenly, his father asked me. 'Akash, what had happened to him? Why is he not saying anything? And why is he lying here? Why is the operation not going on? And if he is well, then why is he not uttering anything?'

I was dumbstruck after seeing their pain.

His father cried, 'Doctors, where are you?' And he started moving outside the room.

I stopped him, and I replied, 'Uncle, he is no longer with us. He is dead.' As I said this, they became dumbstruck, and his mother fainted. I was stunned to see his mother faint. I immediately rushed outside the room, brought some water, and sprinkled it over her face. After some time, she was fine, and she regained consciousness. But in her heart, she was shattered. I understood that losing a son is a big loss that can't be recovered by anyone.

As I was leaving the room, Rishabh's dad stopped me and started asking me about the whole incident, when and how it happened. I explained to him the entire incident, and I left the room and went to Sumant, who was in the same position as I saw him in the beginning. It seemed that someone had made him into a statue, but I understood his love for Rishabh. He was his best friend, and losing a best friend is very excruciating for the loved ones. He was in a very shocked condition.

As I touched Sumant's shoulder to console him, I heard someone calling me. I turned back, and I saw they were Anshika and Ananya. As they reached near to us, I saw tears on their faces also, and there were only questions coming from their mouths.

'How are they? And where are they?'

'Akansha has been admitted to ICU.'

'What?'

'Yes.'

'And what about Rishabh?'

I didn't say any answer to this question, seeing their tears and their panic after hearing the word *ICU*. I remained silent, but suddenly, they cried together in a loud voice, and they again asked me.

'Where is Rishabh?'

Sumant and I both got fearful after listening to their loud voices, and I replied to them that Rishabh was no more.

'What? What the hell are you saying? How do you know that?' Ananya cried.

'Yah, I know what I am saying, and it's true. Actually, after the collision with a truck, he fell down, and the truck's back wheel ran over his stomach. There and then he was dead. Actually, it was a spot death, and I even checked his pulse and breathing there on the road. I came to know that he was dead, but I didn't say it to anyone else. I thought that if I will say it, then Sumant may become more livid towards me. That's why I remained silent, and when Rishabh was brought to the hospital, the doctor declared him dead.'

'But where is he?' Anshika asked me.

I pointed to the room, and they rushed to see Rishabh. I shouted again to remind them also not to remove the whole bed sheet and only to remove it from his face because I knew that if they removed the whole sheet, then they will get fearful as well as panicked to see his damaged body. Anshika listened to me and went in.

After saying this, I turned around and saw the parents of Akansha. I was able to identify her mom only because I saw her once when she came to school to pick up Akansha after school. They also have the same body posture. They even asked all those same questions which was asked by Rishabh's parents and friends. I relayed to them the entire incident. And even I requested her father to submit the fees. After this, her father submitted the fees, and they even went to Rishabh's room to see his corpse. At last, we all were waiting outside the ICU. The red light was on; everybody was crying and praying to God for Akansha to get well soon.

After an hour, the red light got turned off, and we all were eager to know the result. The door opened, and the doctor came out.

'Who are her parents?' the doctor asked.

Her father approached the doctor.

'See, the operation is successful, but I cannot say about her. She is still in danger, and moreover, she had lost a lot of her blood. She requires blood. I have tested her blood group. She requires an O positive blood. You all decide who has O positive blood and who can give it. And ha, it's very important. She needs blood within half an hour. Otherwise, her condition may become more critical. So please, be fast, and come to me, whoever wants to give it.'

'Doctor, I am ready to give blood to my daughter. We have the same blood type,' her father said.

I became a little bit happy to know that blood was available very easily and that her father was ready to give his because in many cases, I have heard that blood was not available within the members of the family. And in some cases, blood was not available even in the blood banks also, and in such cases, the patient dies.

But after ten minutes, I became a little bit anxious when I came to know that the doctors have denied taking the blood of her father because he was suffering from some disease. And her mother was also suffering from the same disease. She also went to get checked, and the doctor also denied her giving her blood. Her father approached me with tears on his eyes and requested me to get connected with a blood bank, and he even tried to give me a bundle of 100 rupees, which I denied to take.

'Don't think that I am giving the money to you for the help which you have given. That was your responsibility because you are a friend, and you are even like my son. This money is for blood which you will buy from the blood bank.'

I liked the words of her father saying I was like his son.

'Uncle, I will give blood to your daughter. We also have the same blood type.'

As I said this, a smile came over his face, and he blessed me a lot. He even said I was a deity who is helping his daughter.

'Uncle, I am your son, not a deity.'

But then he replied, 'Whenever the worst situation comes, if no one is there to help, if all gates are closed, then remember the deity gate is always open, and the deity is always there to aid you in the end. And that's why I said you are a deity because in the end you are aiding us to save my daughter.'

I thanked her father for giving me so much respect, and I even told him that it was my responsibility to save her because she was my friend. After saying this, I met the doctor. He checked my blood and accepted me to give my blood to Akansha. The doctor and I entered the ICU. I lay on the other bed near Akansha's bed as per the doctor's suggestions to give blood to her. But before putting the injection into me, at first he checked Akansha, and while he was checking, I saw the anxiousness and sweat on his face.

I asked him, 'What happened to her? Is anything serious?'

He replied to me in a slow voice that she was no more. I was stunned to hear this, and tears even started rolling down my cheeks also. I got up from the bed and started waddling towards the door. As I opened the door, everybody started looking at me because everybody was agog to know the result. But as they saw my pale face with tears rolling down my cheeks, they became tense, and there was only one question in their mouths.

'What happened?'

I replied to them that she was no longer with us. As I said this, everybody rushed inside the room, and there was only one sound which came from there—it was of their crying. I started thinking of how that day, with our plans to enjoy the picnic and console Akansha that I didn't love her, killed two of our beloved friends and even on the same day— one in the morning, spot death, and another in the night. I had never imagined that this could also happen. For me and my friends, it was just an extremely unpleasant day which could never be forgotten in our whole lives.

Ten Years Later

Somehow, I completed my CA and I started doing a job in a good MNC company. But I shattered the dream of the cricket coach who had financed me to get educated in an English-medium school with the hope that I could learn English and become a good cricketer who had a good command of English. But later on, I gained knowledge that India required efficient entrepreneurs to remove poverty. I decided to be an entrepreneur.

And to be an entrepreneur, I started doing jobs so as to acquire large amounts of money. A few years later, I started my own business, and then I met Anshika, who was already a surgical doctor. And some few months later, I got married to Anshika. Finally, after enjoying our married life for two months, Anshika and I decided to recall our childhood life, and to recall it, I thought to call Sumant and Ananya only because Rishabh and Akansha were no longer with us.

I made a call to them to invite them. Both their numbers were switched off. But luckily, I knew the address of Sumant. I went there to invite him, and he was even there at the same home. I invited him, and I even asked him about Ananya, but he ignored me and said that he did not know about her. I informed Anshika that Ananya will not be with us, and it was bad news for us because sharing childhood life with the absence of even one friend from the remaining two friends who were still alive was useless.

The next day, the bell rang, and Sumant arrived along with Ananya. This was a very nice surprise for us. Anshika and I asked Sumant from where he brought Ananya. He replied that to give us a surprise, he didn't tell me about her. Finally, without even wasting time, we started talking about of our childhood days. And even to recall our school life, we started playing the truth-or-dare game, which was the popular game in our childhood days.

While playing the game, I remembered wanting to know the reason behind the serious talk between Anshika and Ananya when I saw them talking in Water Parks. And as my chance came to ask the question to Anshika, I asked the same question to her, and I came to know that on our first Valentine's Day, Anshika got a message from Rishabh that he loved her but she didn't reply to him and she was just taking tips from Ananya on how to console him.

But in the next round, Anshika got the chance to ask a question to me. And she asked me the same question because she even saw me and Sumant talking about something serious. I said the entire truth to Anshika.

'On that Valentine's Day, I got a message from Akansha that she loved me, and I even replied to her that I also loved her, but it was accidentally because the number was not known to me and I thought that you were messaging me knowingly just to make a fool out of me. That was why I replied to that number. And I even thought that you might have been kidding with me by changing your SIM card. That was why I sent that message.'

And I even told Anshika that Sumant and I were discussing about this matter and that I was also taking tips on how to console Akansha. After saying the truth, I was a little bit fearful that she may become annoyed. But nothing like that happened.

And in the next chance I got, I asked a question to Sumant. And I asked him the same question on how he brought Ananya here, and he replied that Anshika and I had already given the answer. We became doubtful, and then he said that my whole story was known to him and Anshika's whole story was known to Ananya.

'In our childhood, we both knew that I was the best friend of yours and she was the best friend of hers. We didn't say anything to you and Anshika, and by hiding from you both, we used to meet each other. I used to share your personal views with Ananya, and she used to share Anshika's views with me. And these meetings later changed into romantic dates. We married each other, and we were even not able to call anyone.'

This news made me shocked that they were married, but we were blissful to know that our childhood friends later turned into each other's spouses.

The next year, Anshika gave birth to twins—one boy and one girl. We named them Rishabh and Akansha not because they proposed to us or because they were a boyfriend or girlfriend to us but just because they were true friends to us.